# AVA'S LIFE

## Eyewitness Accounts of God's Grace and Power

By AVA N. LEE

Published by Purpose Books, P.O. Box 15561, Little Rock, AR 72231



Printed in the United States of America

Library of Congress Control Number: 2023914476

Please consider requesting that a copy of this book be purchased by your local library system.

ISBN: 978-1-7331248-4-3

# TABLE OF CONTENTS

Introduction.......1
Life Before My Birth.......4
The 1930s.......13
The 1940s.......53
The 1950s.......94
The 1960s.......129
The 1970s.......147
The 1980s.......171
The 1990s.......196
2000 to Present.......202

# INTRODUCTION

I was born just before the depression in October 1929 in cold northern Indiana. My family loved God, or at least thought they did. But they did not know Him.

My parents moved about 100 miles south of Gary, where I was born, to a poor little sandhill and 40-acre swamp. They dug out a living with seven children and nothing else.

I was taught from babyhood about this great big, wonderful God who lived way off in Heaven somewhere. He was supposed to be everywhere, but I couldn't see Him or feel Him. He had a son who came down here for a while and died to save us. I wish I could have been here to meet Him. I wanted to know Him.

When I was about four, my two older sisters walked with me to the little country Church of Christ. I was hungry for God, but on the other hand, I really didn't know what I wanted.

I remember one Sunday when people sang "Who Will Follow Jesus." I listened, then declared, "Lord, I will if You will show me how." Daddy and Mother also wanted to know how to follow Him. Daddy knew that there must be more to serving God than just living a good, clean life.

I wanted to go every week, but they wouldn't let my sister Juanita and I walk there alone.

We started attending house meetings with people who were often called Holy Rollers, Jesus-Name-Only folks, and more. We didn't know what we were getting into. I was nine the first time I went. I watched every move. I was hungry for God.

Was this what I had been seeking?

Yes, it was exactly what I needed.

Thank you, Jesus! Four days before I turned 10, I received the Holy Ghost and my life was never the same.

Wherefore seeing we also are compassed about with so great a cloud of witnesses. (Hebrews 12:1)

# CHAPTER 1

## Life Before My Birth

# There is a God

Daddy told me of a time before I was born when an atheist man on the streets somewhere in Illinois screamed, "There is no God. If there is a God, let him strike me dead now. See! I'm not dead. I told you. There is no God." The man screamed it from the streets for a long time.

When he finally turned to go home, a gnat flew in his eye. He tried to get it out, but it kept working its way farther into his eyeball. He cried because it hurt so badly. After a while, they took him to the hospital, but doctors couldn't find anything. He still cried in pain.

The man died. An autopsy revealed that the little gnat had found its way into the brain where God had sent it.

Definite proof that there is a God.

# Baby with Horns

About the time my oldest brother was born, there was a man in town selling Bibles from house to house. He went to the house of a woman who was soon to have a baby. She was hostile.

"No," she shouted. "I don't want one of those things in my home. I would rather have the devil in my house."

She then slammed the door in his face.

She gave birth to a baby boy a few weeks later. The baby had horns about an inch long. As the baby grew, he got meaner and meaner. My folks moved away and did not know what became of him. Daddy said the boy always wore a cap to hide his horns, but it didn't hide his disposition.

# Misplaced Baby

Mother and Daddy lived in Illinois when a bad tornado danced across the landscape. High winds blew before the storm hit.

An older man stepped outside the barn for something, and the wind took his hat. Angry, he said, "Well, ---- blow." The wind picked him up about 10 feet against the side of the barn. Then he slid back down on his feet. That time, he just said, "huh."

Then the real tornado hit and caused a lot of damage. No one was hurt, but a little girl went missing. Everyone frantically searched the remains of the house. Someone found a little toddler in a cornfield just outside Lomax, eight miles away. No one knew her name and she was too little to tell anyone. She cried for her mama but was not hurt at all.

God works in mysterious ways.
Sets his footsteps on the sea.
He rides on every storm.
Just maybe with a baby in his arms.

# Glenna

When Glenna, Mother's fifth child, was about three and a half, she came down to breakfast, happy as usual. When most all were seated around the table, Glenna started screaming. Mother couldn't do anything with her.

One of the bigger children ran for Grandma Norris a little way down the street. Grandma came running. At some point, the doctor was called. Glenda started vomiting.

"Oh, just a little upset stomach," the doctor said. "She'll be all right in a bit."

But she fell unconscious and died that evening.

Grandma helped Mother clean up the mess Glenna made when she vomited. Everything it touched turn bright purple. They couldn't bleach it out, so they burned everything it stained.

The next winter, Daddy was short on garage work, so he decided to develop some pictures. He had a picture developing machine in a small room upstairs which was off limits for children. The rolls of film had to be placed in water with some kind of tablet dissolved in the water.

After developing the pictures, Mother took the water downstairs and threw it in the snow which then turned bright purple. It was then we surmised that Glenna had mettled in that room, got a capsule and swallowed it. We believe that's what killed her.

The doctor had cited Glenda’s appendix as the cause of her death.

Daddy blamed himself. He didn’t know those capsules were poison.

# The Tramp

My grandmother Norris did laundry for rich people to support her six children. She scrubbed the clothes on the washboard and then boiled the white ones to make them whiter. One day, a tramp appeared at the back door.

"I'm hungry," the tramp said. "Could you give me a bite to eat?"

Grandma said she would get him some food and told him to stand outside the door and wait. When she started to close the door, he stuck his foot in it and would not allow her to close it. Grandma had white clothes on the stove boiling, so she grabbed a large dipper of boiling water, threw it in the tramp's face and then issued an ultimatum.

"You get out of town by the time my husband gets home from work," Grandma said. "If he can find you, he will kill you.

When Grandpa got home, he took his gun and hunted the town over, but no tramp could be found.

# A Sick Spoiled Brat

Arlo was four when the doctor diagnosed him with typhoid fever. His fever rose in the daytime and fell at night. I think Mother said the lowest was 94 degrees and the highest 104. Mother bathed him in cool water in the daytime and warm water at night.

When the doctor came, he said the fever couldn't have been that low. He wouldn't be here. Mother said, "Doc, I took it three times." That day, it didn't go quite so high, and the next night not quite so low. He couldn't eat solid food but was on the mend.

Sterling was about four months. He was changed and fed and laid down on the floor on a blanket where Juanita played with him.

Arlo couldn't walk and was badly crippled. As he learned to walk, he walked on the side of his foot (ankle bone). The doctor said he also had polio. Mother spoiled Arlo on the days he was well.

When Arlo was about 14, he said, "I wish she had just let me die."

Unthankful and unholy.

# Coal Come Yet?

Mother, Daddy and six children lived in Gary, Indiana. Daddy worked on electric power lines from the east coast to Chicago. He came home and ordered coal before going back to work. He wanted to make sure his family stayed warm. But the coal didn't come.

A family across the street couldn't speak good English but were dependable people. The man of the household watched out for us when Daddy was gone.

"Coal come yet?" the man asked for three days straight.

"No, it hasn't," Mother answered.

Our coal supply was almost gone. What would Mother do?

The neighbor man took Elroy, 13, to an alley where they cut down a tree and carried it in for firewood. They had plenty of wood until the coal came.

Mother always spoke kindly of that nice man who kept us all from freezing to death. Mother never forgot the kindness of people who helped her.

# CHAPTER 2

## The 1930s

# Rain

In 1930, Mother and Daddy moved from Gary, Indiana to 40 acres of swamp, sand hills and scrub brush with seven children. I was five months old. They rented a house up a half-mile lane and started a home. They built a basement and moved into it. We had sand floors. Rats dug under the walls and got inside. Mice ran everywhere. We all learned there was no use complaining. We did with what we had.

In 1939, Jesus came to our house (basement). Things were some better. We got concrete floors. The rats vanished, but we still had mice. And we needed a new roof.

It started raining one church night when Mother stood and asked a question.

"What do you do when it rains?" she asked.

"I suppose you let it rain," Pastor said.

"We have to do more," Mother said. "Our roof leaks and we must hang up kettles and buckets."

She had nails in the rafters to hang the kettles and buckets, so we didn't flood. Soon, we heard, "ping, ping ping" as the water started dripping in the pans.

Oh, the good ol' days. The rain came, but so did God's blessings.

# The Little Vicks Jug

When we were children, we did everything we could to make a few cents to help feed our family. Daddy hauled freight in Illinois and worked hard for very little.

Mother read of a woman who sold baked goods to workers. Robert, 12, begged Mother to bake some cookies or a pie so he could try selling them in town 10 miles away. Elroy and Robert picked up stuff from the city dumps to build bicycles to ride to town.

Mother had enough ingredients to make a dozen cupcakes. She made them, wrapping them separately in waxed paper. She put them in a large shoebox. Robert took the box on his bike and hurried to town.

A group of hard-working men bought them all for 60 cents. Robert used the money to buy what Mother needed and was back home in a little over two hours.

"Hurry, Mommy," Robert said. "Make some more."

Mother vowed to make more the next morning.

Robert was a handsome, happy, friendly chap whom everyone liked. If anyone could sell, Robert could. Mother increased her baking every day. She made pies, cakes, and cookies of every kind. Robert nearly always sold out quickly which helped buy groceries for our family. Nothing fancy, but we had food on the table.

Mother baked for several years before adding garden fresh green onions, red and white radishes, and flowers to also sell in town. I was two years old when all the selling started, and it continued when I was grown.

Mother gave us a Vicks jug in which to carry our money. Sterling made a run to Francesville. When he got home, he realized that he had lost his Vicks jug.

"Mama, when I saw I had lost it, I went back and looked all along the road, but I couldn't find it," Sterling said. "I'm sorry."

"We will get along," Mother said. "Don't worry."

A few weeks later, Daddy walked to town. When he started home, a neighbor picked him up. They were riding along talking when Daddy quickly said, "Stop! Let me out!" The puzzled neighbor stopped. As Daddy got out, he said, "Go on, or wait for me, whichever you want. But I want that Vicks jug."

Note: The little blue Vicks jug is the only thing I know that hasn't changed in 90 years. Oh, they are made of plastic now instead of glass, but they look just the same.

# Pinching Bug

I was maybe three years old when I felt the pain of pinching bugs while playing in the sandhill with my brother Sterling. Mother and the other children were catching chickens in the chicken house to sell. Daddy and the buyer were loading them when I started screaming.

"What's the matter?" he asked.

"Something is biting me under my arm," I yelled.

My dress came off. Daddy grabbed his side cutters and cut off the pinching bug's head. Then he pulled them out one at a time. He handed my dress to me and said, "Go in and get someone to put your dress on." I wasn't big enough to put it on myself. I ran as fast as I could to the house with nothing on but my panties! Daddy, the chicken man, Sterling, and Robert all saw me without my dress.

Juanita dressed me but I wouldn't go back outside. I was too ashamed. We were not saved people. Neither were we "of the world." I knew before I was big enough to dress myself that I needed to keep my body covered.

Now, my great grandson, at nearly four, can come out of the bathroom naked in front of anyone. And I have to close my eyes…and my mouth.

# Ticklish

I was very ticklish. My daddy loved to tickle me. I was about four or five when the tickling made me sick. I pleaded with him to quit, but he didn't. Mother saw there was something wrong with me and stopped him. I was still laughing, but not a regular laugh. I was so sick.

Later, I laughed instead of cried if I hurt myself. I hurt inside. I couldn't help it.

"You've got to stop that," Mother told me.

But I couldn't. I hurt so much inside (man looks on the outside, but God looks on the heart). I eventually got baptized and received the Holy Ghost. Still, I laughed when I or anyone else got hurt.

I remember when Daddy hit his knee with the hammer while working. He passed out cold. I was so scared, yet I laughed. I prayed, but God didn't answer.

In 1947, Juanita's little girl, Wanda, fell from the back seat of the car going about 35 miles per hour. She fell on her face in the middle of the street. A man on the sidewalk ran and picked her up and declared her dead. We all believed she was. My sister had great faith. Juanita asked to be driven to the folks' house 30 miles away. By the time they got there, Wanda was alive. That was all. She was unconscious.

I took one look at her. Her face looked like a hamburger. I started to laugh before going around the garage. My heart cried out to God. I prayed until I really started crying.

"God, please take it all away," I said. "How can I hurt so and still laugh?"

After about an hour, I felt relief come. I went back to the car. They had all gone inside. I found Wanda lying on my bed and Juanita praying beside her.

The next morning, her face was scabbed over, and she was awake. Three days later, the scabs fell off, leaving no scars.

I no longer laugh when someone gets hurt, but I usually laugh when I hurt myself, even when tears fall.

And I'm no longer ticklish.

**Wanda just a few weeks before falling out of the car. She survived the fall.**

# Ben: God is so Good to Me

Ben was different from most of us. Most of us were shy. But not Ben. He wanted to do everything for himself, and he wanted everyone to see that he could. When he was two, he didn't want to be rocked in the rocker. He wanted everyone to see he could do it for himself.

Ben was good at whatever he decided to do, but he wanted to do the deciding. He wanted to be the best. If he didn't know something, it wasn't worth knowing anyhow.

The girls all took music lessons. He could play better by ear on anything he tried (except flute). As a young man, he usually played the saxophone. When he was middle age, he took to the accordion which is mostly all he plays now. Ben didn't get in church until he was about 19, so his younger talents were wasted. He really could sing.

When he was about seven, he sang the song, "There's Something Better than Gold." He was small for his age and had a lisp. People thought that was cute. They would get him to sing, "Oh yeth, Oh yeth, Oh yeth" (yes there's something better than gold). Everyone loved Bennie.

Mildred was boarding with a minster's family who wanted her to take Bennie to their home for a week. They really enjoyed him, even though he was a picky eater. He refused to eat corn beef hash one night because he was accustomed to potatoes and gravy. He took a small bite, pushed it back, and said, "I think this stuff was made for the pig slop." Mildred was so embarrassed. But the family thought it funny.

Ben had three bad accidents when he was older. No one expected him to live after two of those. He was unable to speak after one accident.

"He can't make it this time," the doctor said.

Ben's son, Melvin, took his dad's hand.

"Dad, if you can hear me, look at me and squeeze my hand."

One eye was swollen shut. The other opened slowly and turned very slowly towards Melvin. Then Ben very faintly squeezed his hand. Melvin turned to the doctor and said, "Dad will make it."

Ben now walks with two canes. He can stand and scoot his feet across the floor, but he says it hurts terribly. The canes help take the weight off his legs. He lives alone, dresses himself, does his own laundry at the laundromat, and still gets on his knees to pray. I worry about him when the weather is cold, and the roads are slick. Once he fell in the snow-filled yard and couldn't get up. He called his son eight miles away to come and get him up.

I think he has some crazy ideas. He thinks I do. We love each other and get along fine.

He's the best and only brother I have left.

# Ava

Arlo had about six operations on his right foot and leg so he could walk. We were 100 miles from the hospital and had no car. I remember Daddy taking him on a bicycle one time. Every time they dismissed Arlo, he brought the rest of us something we didn't want: measles, chicken pox, and more.

Arlo brought us whooping cough in 1933, just four months after Ben was born. I was already a sickly child, and the cough turned into rickets.

They carried me out, picked Mother's only lily, took my picture, and carried me back in the house. I still remember it. They thought I wouldn't make it that time. That's been over 88 years ago and I'm still here.

**My family snapped this photo while I was ill with whooping cough. I lived to tell about it.**

# Arlo

As a child, I hated my brother Arlo. I didn't realize I hated him until I received the Holy Ghost.

He was three when he had the accident that caused him to get typhoid fever and polio at the same time. This caused older people to spoil him rotten. He was six years older than me, but he was mean to me. I had one little China dog about an inch high that my Grandma Miller gave to me. Arlo would get my dog and hide it or put it up so high that I couldn't get it. At that time, I had no other toy.

Arlo was badly crippled. Because of his condition, everyone spoiled him except his brothers and sisters. At that time, he had three older and four younger siblings at home.

I was always very afraid of Arlo. He hurt me many times. He lied on me and got me in trouble many times. We always said, "He lied when the truth would have served him better."

He pinched me, pulled my hair, tripped me, and more. He usually lied about it or said it was an accident. If we could prove it, then he would be punished. But he would never be punished severely because of his crippled condition and his near-death experience. Sometimes it was better to not tell on him because he would do something worse if we did.

But Jesus came to our house.

In 1939, we got acquainted with what the people of the world called "holy rollers." In August, Daddy, Mother, Juanita, and Arlo were baptized in the precious name of Jesus, and they were all filled with the Holy Ghost. The hate left me, but the fear of Arlo didn't. Arlo was 15 at the time. I was baptized and got the Holy Ghost about eight weeks later in October.

Spring came. There was joy in our home and our family. Arlo seemed to be even good to me sometimes, but the orneriness never left him.

Daddy bought an old tractor to help on the farm. After several operations, Arlo was able to run the tractor. He could walk well now. One day, he wanted to teach me to drive the tractor. I didn't want to learn. I was still afraid of him. But now he had Jesus. I had to love and trust him.

Arlo finally got me on the tractor, put it in low gear, and showed me how to turn the way I needed to go. He showed me everything but how to stop. He left it in my hands and jumped off the back. He then went around about 12 feet in front of the tractor and laid down. I turned the wheel. He got up and laid a little closer. I turned it back the other way. He kept doing it, getting closer every time. As usual, I started crying.

What can I do? I can't kill my brother. I started really praying. I remembered that Daddy pushed a pedal to stop the car. I tried it and it worked. I had to hold the clutch in until Arlo got on.

He always said he was going to let me run over him. What was he doing? Trying to kill himself and make me do the job? He never got me back on the tractor again and I realized I still couldn't trust him. He went on through life, trying to hold God's hand with one hand and the devil with the other. As a child, I never told anyone about the incident with the tractor.

A couple years later, Arlo was going to pick up the Rose children for church. Mother told me to get dressed and go with him. I was afraid, but when Mother tells you do something, you do it. Arlo told me to stay in the car for a minute so he could talk to me.

"The Lord told me you are not right with Him," Arlo told me. "You did something that you need to repent of."

"What is it?" I asked.

"You should know," he responded.

"But I don't. I'm living as close to God as I know how."

"God didn't tell me that," Arlo said.

I cried as usual. When the altar call came, I was the first one there, I repented with all my heart. Arlo came and put his hand on my back and prayed for me.

The next morning, Mother asked why I had gone to the altar. "Have you done something?" she asked.

"Not that I know of," I said. "But Arlo said God showed him that I had so I just wanted to be sure."

"Well, he's a great one to talk the way that he lives," Mother said.

I never knew what she meant, but I never had to go with him again.

# Boy on a Bike

When I was a little girl, probably about five, we went to town on a dark evening. Streetlights were only "uptown" and there were probably about four lights in the whole town. We were at the edge of town and Daddy didn't seem to know where he needed to go.

I always stood in the back behind Daddy, just as close to him as I could get. Mother held baby Ben in the front seat. Daddy started to make a left turn. The car lights were very poor, and it seemed awfully dark. Turn lights were unheard of back then.

Just as he started turning, Mother grabbed his arm and screamed, "Boy on a bike!" The dim headlights picked up the boy's white shirt. He was crossing the street onto which Daddy turned.

Daddy stopped just in time. He sat there a long time, thanking Mother for saving him from running over the child. They should have both been thanking God, but they didn't yet know Him.

God was ever watching over us.

I praise Him!

# My Very First Start for God

I was about two when we moved into our basement home. For the next seven or eight years, I can only remember going to church four times, except for the Little White Church on the Hill. Twice I went with a neighbor because Juanita wanted me to go. It was a Methodist church. Juanita loved church as I did.

I overheard Daddy and Mother talking.

"We promised the children they could make their own choice as to where they go to church." Mother said.

"But Methodist?" Daddy said. "They don't even believe in baptism. We know that's not right."

In my heart, I knew if Daddy said it wasn't right, then it wasn't right.

"I ain't goin' no more!" I said.

The next Sunday, Juanita told me it was time to get ready for church.

"I ain't goin'," I said. "I don't want to."

Inside, I wanted to go to church, but not if it was the wrong place.

I remember going with Daddy and Mother once when Hazel was a baby, and I was six. Daddy always lived a good life. No drinking, no smoking, no bad language. He used a lot of slang and unnecessary words like "phooey," “fiddlesticks,” “man alive,” and “boy, oh boy.” I can’t name them all. The Bible says we must give account of every idol word (Matthew 12:36).

Daddy and Mother went to the Church of Christ, but the one with music. They couldn’t go much because the family didn’t have clothes. Then, we went to the Seventh Day Adventist, but the Little White Church on the Hill is where I wanted to go. One morning, Mildred, Juanita and I walked there. I just wanted to go to church. They always sang such beautiful songs, and I sang them the way I thought they did. Instead of singing “Brighten the Corner Where You Are,” I sang “Right in the Corner Where you Are.” I sang “Bringing in the Cheese,” instead of “Bringing in the Sheaves.”

And then there was the song “Who Will Follow Jesus?”

“I will,” I said in my heart. “Jesus, show me the way and I will follow.”

That was over 85 years ago. I’m still asking. Show me the way more perfectly, and I will follow.

# Caraway Seed

Back in 1935, times were still very hard. Food for our family was scarce, and really good food was not to be had at all.

One morning, the neighbors across the road brought over Doris, their little girl who was about our age. The mother asked if we could keep Doris while they conducted business in town.

That was fine. Neighbors did that back then. About 11:30, Mother said, "I don't know what to do. I don't have anything to fix for lunch." She rummaged through the cabinets and found nothing but caraway seed.

She put some water on the stove to boil with the caraway seed in it. It smelled so good. She mixed flour, baking powder, salt, and a little sugar. Using enough milk to moisten the flour, she dropped it by the spoonful into the boiling water mixture. I remember it tasted so good.

We asked mother to make it again, but there was no more caraway seed.

Jesus provided for us long before we knew Him.

# Burned Hands

To me, burns are the worst kind of pain. I was a very small girl, but I loved to help Mother with whatever she was doing. I was probably more trouble than I was worth. About like it is now. I asked what I could do to help. The answer was usually "sit down and look pretty."

"I can't," I said. "I looked in the mirror."

Mother, no matter how busy, always took the time to show me what to do to help. My precious mother was the best in the whole world. She seemed to be very busy one particular morning when I was about six.

"Mommy, can I help you?"

"Yes, honey," she said. "You can stir the oats."

In those days, there was no such thing as quick oats. Oats had to be boiled for 20 minutes and stirred all the time to keep them from sticking and burning. I took the spoon and started stirring. I stood on something to make me high enough to stir.

Arlo had his back to me, sitting at the table playing dominoes. I must have touched Arlo's arm or back or something. He elbowed me and I fell flat on the palms of my hands on the red-hot stove. Someone grabbed the Unguentine, a salve Mother kept for burns. Mother salved my burns by putting my palms together and wrapping them. I wondered why. I always thought it was an odd way to wrap burns. After thinking about it all the years later, I concluded that she was conserving salve. She knew she would need a lot by the time my hands would be well.

I remember Mother holding my hands, crying, and walking the floor with me from room to room before stopping to rock me. Then Daddy rocked me while Mother finished breakfast. What I remember most of the whole tragedy was how much they cared for me and loved me.

It was about three years before Jesus came to our house, and I didn't hear anybody pray.

I had scars on my hands for about 12 years.

# Christmas

When I was a small child, Mother and Daddy went all out for Christmas: Santa Claus, tree, candy, popcorn, gifts. Mother made us girls new dresses and the boys new shirts if she could get the material. They never borrowed money for Christmas but labored hard to make it a happy time.

Candy was weighed in the stores by the pound in brown paper sacks. No candy came wrapped except boxed chocolates. I remember the store clerk weighing orange slices on balance scales.

If the hard candy was left in a warm room, it became one solid lump. Daddy got a hammer and screwdriver to break it apart after Christmas. Daddy tried to have a three-gallon pan full of candy. We would have all we wanted on Christmas day.

We went to the woods and cut a cedar tree. We didn't have pines growing that far north. After this special day, it could be used for a fence post. They made a frame with 2x4s and fastened it with nails. The smaller children cut strips of paper from the Sears Roebuck catalog and glued them together with flour paste to make chains for decorating the tree. One year, Mildred made an angel for the top. We made popcorn chains and ate the popcorn off the tree. Another year, we had a Santa at the top, not knowing the truth. Mildred, Juanita, and Arlo made stars, bells and snowflakes to decorate.

Mother and Daddy told us that Santa wasn't real, but Santa always came dressed in a red suit. It seemed Daddy always missed seeing Santa. We knew it was a man dressed who came to see us. One year, we had fresh snow. Sterling and I tracked him a little way.

We didn't know that the celebration day had been changed three times and the birthday of Jesus was not recorded. We didn't know. Jesus was not at all pleased with our celebration.

But Jesus came to our house.

Not to spend a day or two, but the rest of our lives. First, Daddy read Jeremiah 10. Out with the Christmas tree. Then, he took Galatians 4:10-11 to heart, and we stopped observing most holidays.

Hazel liked to study. She spent a whole day at the library. When she came home, she quit celebrating New Year's Day, Valentine's Day, Easter, St. Patrick's Day, and Christmas. We still had Mother's Day, Father's Day, Independence Day, and Thanksgiving.

Many years later, Hazel and I worked for Joe Crain at his chicken and egg farm. Christmas came.

"Won't you come in and eat with us and celebrate," Mr. Crain asked.

Of course, we said no. Before we finished gathering the morning eggs, Mrs. Crain brought us each a plate of Christmas dinner. We thanked her and went on running eggs. She put the plates down and went back inside. When we came to a stopping place with the eggs, we thanked God for the food and started eating. Neither of us felt right about it.

Everything our hearts could wish for was on that plate. We were hungry. As we were about to finish eating, Hazel said, "If they bid you to a feast and say, 'This is offered to an idol,' eat not." We finished our plates, not knowing what we should do.

The next Christmas, I worked and lived alone. I didn't keep much food in the house. I ran eight miles into town to get me a hamburger or something. All restaurants, grocery stores and most gas stations were closed. The town of Palatka was dead. Finally, I found a 7-11 store where I bought a big chicken thigh. I ate it while driving back to work. It was too greasy and refused to stay down. Since that time, I stay home at Christmas, eat the same as other days, and I don't give Christmas gifts.

I don't want to hurt anyone, but I must do as I feel God has led me. I'm not perfect, but I'm still trying to be.

# Big and Little Brothers

Ben loved his big brother, Robert. We were not yet in church, but God was surely taking care of us. We believed in God the Father and Jesus his Son. But we knew nothing about the Holy Ghost. That hadn't been given to us yet.

Ben (affectionately called "Bennie" then) was riding around with Robert in his truck on our little 40-acre farm. Bennie was about four or five at the time. Robert was a wild driver which Bennie loved. When Robert made a wild circle into the yard, the truck door flew open, and Ben rolled out. The truck ran over his hand and his hair.

When he got up crying, he said, "You pulled my hair!"

Ben is now 90.

# I'm So Cold

As a small child, I loved my brother Sterling who was 20 months older than me. He was two years and one month old when we moved from Gary to the 40 acres in 1930.

I was not healthy and very small (I sure outgrew it). I didn't start school until I was nearly seven. Sterling and I walked to and from school together a mile and a half.

We had syrup buckets to carry our lunch. One day, it turned very cold. I had mittens but it seems I was always cold. Sterling stopped in the road. Of course, I stopped, too. He took my lunch bucket, tightened my coat around my neck, fixed my stocking cap and scarf, pulled off his homemade mittens, and put them over the top of mine. I tried to stop him out of concern that he would get cold. He said, "Just wait."

He picked up the lunch buckets ran one handle on each arm, shoved his hands his pocket, and said, "Come on, let's go home."

I remember my school life as nearly always cold. Sometimes the teacher would be building the fire in the wood heating stove when we got to school.

Cold in winter. Just so cold.

# Disobedience and the Penalty

We had an old Thore washing machine. We had always scrubbed on a scrub board until our fingers were sore. Even the little ones knew what it was to scrub.

Mother was happy to get the washer, but it was dangerous. It could take a hand or entire arm if anyone ever got a finger caught in the wringer. We were warned to never touch the wringer.

I was about eight, old enough to mind. Mother was outside hanging clothes on the line. Juanita was in the far bedroom sewing. I started to go outside and saw the wringer running. It had soap bubbles on it where Mother had wrung the clothes from the washer to the rinse water. I stopped to play in the soap bubbles. Me? Yes, me. I certainly wasn't a perfect child, even though I did want to be. I didn't want to sin. But what could be wrong with playing in soap bubbles? I wanted to break the bubbles as the wringer went around.

Ouch! That pinched me. I jerked back. My thumb was bigger. It wouldn't go between the rollers, but it grabbed my thumb (Just like the devil to say, "I gotcha now").

I pulled. I screamed. I pulled. I screamed. Juanita knew what I had done. She ran and fell on the release lever and turned me loose.

Mother heard my screaming from the clothesline. She blamed herself for not shutting off the wringer. No! A thousand times no! No one was to blame but me. Why won't kids just mind?

The penalty? All the meat and skin were pulled off the inside of my thumb. We couldn't afford a doctor. Daddy and Mother pushed the bloody mess back together to almost look like a thumb.

After more than 80 years, my thumb is still flat and wide with a scar about two inches long. For years, it would get very sore, and I would pull out the scar tissue where it bends at the knuckle. Did I complain? No! I just reminded myself that this was a result of disobedience.

Our spiritual life is much like the earthly. Jesus is our example and our help in time of trouble. I had Mother, Daddy, and Sister. We have Jesus, who is our heavenly Father, Mother, Sister, and Brother. He gives us pastors, teachers, and leaders to help us go right. He tells us to "love not the world."

Do we pay attention? No. We'll be punished certainly.

Do we want to play in the soap bubbles of sin and have the scars of sin for life? My scar serves as a reminder that disobedience to Mother or God does not pay.

# Peer Pressure

This is a story I know I must write. I have refrained from doing so because I am so ashamed of what I did. But I must write about it.

I think I was seven, trying to live for God but not knowing Him. My teacher, Augusta Walknuts, brought coloring books to school and passed them out to some of the children. She left me out. The next day, she brought more to different children, still leaving me out. I finally told her that I wanted one, so she brought me one the next day.

It was not a pretty one and had fewer pages than the others.

"You know these are a nickel," she said as she handed it to me.

I had no nickel. Never had a nickel and figured I never would. She laid it on my desk. What could I do? I couldn't tell Mama what I had done. She didn't have the money for food, much less junk like coloring books.

The next day, Mrs. Walknuts wanted her nickel. Every day, I conveniently "forgot" to bring it. One sin leads to another. School was about to be out. I had to do something quick. I knew where Mommy kept her money can, but there was usually nothing in it.

Everyone was outside at home when I got a chair to reach the little can. A nickel and a penny. That's all Mommy had. I took the nickel. Stole it, I did! I took it to school the next morning and paid for the coloring book. But I couldn't take it home because everyone seemed to know that coloring books were a nickel. Mommy would know I stole her nickel if she discovered it missing from the can.

I couldn't leave the coloring book at school. We were to clean out everything from our desks. I decided to walk home alone from school and drop it in a deep place in the roadside ditch. I thought all was well, but Momma still missed her nickel.

Elroy was a thief, stealing everything he wanted. But he was now an adult and had left home. I was the eighth child. Of course, I would not think of stealing.

Mother got us all together.

"I have a nickel missing," she said. "Someone took it out of my money can. I had a nickel and a penny. The penny is there. The nickel is gone. Someone had to take it. I hope I don't have another thief."

They all denied (rightfully) taking it. I was not accused or even thought about. But oh, my heart was heavy.

I coveted, lied and stole. Sin was piling up!

Then Jesus came. I was nearly 10. I was baptized in the name of Jesus. The load was lifted. I went to Mother and told her what I had done and the load I had carried over two years. She was most concerned about me throwing a new coloring book away.

That was such a waste.

# Mildred

Mildred left home at 20. She was tired of dirt floors, dirty young'uns, and not enough of anything to go around. She was tired of it all. She and Robert had another fuss. She packed up her little blue truck and marched down the road to a "better" life.

Two years later, in 1939, Juanita was preparing to marry. Daddy hunted and traced Mildred to Indianapolis, 100 miles south of home. They sent her a wedding invitation. She came. She had climbed a step or two up the ladder of success, but she had had many setbacks in two years.

When Mildred came home, she came in contact with the church people, which really got her thinking.

Two weeks after the wedding, John, Mother, and Juanita got the Holy Ghost. Mother started writing to Mildred, telling her everything that was happening in our house and in our lives. Without notice, Mildred came home for a visit over the weekend. She and Mother were talking.

"Are you going to get baptized?" Mother asked.

"What do you suppose I came home for?" Mildred asked.

Mildred got baptized, went back to Indianapolis, found a church that believed in Jesus' name baptism, and received the Holy Ghost. But that church had a woman pastor. None of us knew any better.

Mildred had a beautiful gold watch. She had gone hungry to meet the layaway payments on it. While raising her hands to seek the Holy Ghost, she said the watch burned her arm. She jerked it off, threw it, then got the Holy Ghost.

There were a couple good brothers in the church to whom God was speaking. Bro. James Petty and Bro. Larson felt the Lord wanted them to hold a street revival. The woman pastor, Sis. Spillman, said no. God kept speaking to the men and they held street meetings for a week. Several were baptized (at Spillman's church), filled with the Holy Ghost, and were coming to the church from the street meetings.

When Sis. Spillman heard they held the services against her orders, she made all who attended sit in the back seat for six months. Mildred was one of them. They were not allowed to testify or take any part in the service. They all obeyed her, rejoicing that they obeyed God.

As soon as the six months expired, those who were involved left the church and started the Bible Church with Bro. Petty as pastor. Attendance increased steadily while Spillman's decreased.

It pays to obey God rather than wo(man).

# Sterling's Fun

Sterling found fun in the big oak tree swing. The tree branched into two trees about three feet from the ground. Daddy put a heavy rope swing on a large high limb. That was our play yard. I loved it, but I didn't want to swing high.

Sometimes, Sterling pushed me in the swing. He was really a good brother to me. He would swing standing up and then jump out. He loved to do it. Daddy found out he was doing it and ordered him to stop.

Arlo couldn't jump because he was crippled. One day, Sterling was swinging very high. Arlo dared him to jump. Sterling jumped and broke the arches in both feet. He couldn't walk for over a month.

Daddy took our swing down, punishing us all.

Another example of how disobedience does not pay.

# I Was Missing

I was probably about 9 when the Stephensons came over one evening. Louise wanted to take me home for the night, but Daddy said a flat "No!" Daddy believed children needed to be in their own home at night.

When they left our house that night around 10 or 11, I was nowhere to be found. My family looked the house over and looked outside. Daddy thought Louise had slipped me away.

Sterling eventually found me fast asleep on a partial brick wall behind the homemade furnace. I had found a warm spot. I was always cold.

Wow! I almost got a whipping for not going to bed to sleep. Daddy loved me so, and he was so scared when I was missing.

# Didn’t Want to be Trapped

We had been going to house meetings for weeks before Pastor Charles Duncan came to give a Bible study. Daddy, Mother nor Juanita could understand One-God and Jesus-name baptism. That doctrine wasn’t taught at the Seventh Day Adventist Church that we had been attending.

Daddy asked Forest Crawford (the man who got us to attend the Seventh Day Adventist Church) to come to the Bible study and ask questions.

“I want the Bible study to be between you and Mr. Crawford,” Daddy told Bro. Duncan. “I don’t want to talk. I can get more out of it by just listening.”

During the lesson, Bro. Duncan read the scripture John 5:43, “I am come in my Father’s name…”

“What name did He come in?” Pastor asked.

“Christ,” Forest said.

“No,” Pastor said. “Christ is not a name. What name did He come in?”

“Lord,” Forest said.

“No,” the pastor said. “Lord is not a name.”

Then, Mother and Daddy both shouted at the same time, “I see it!”

After the meeting ended, Mother asked Forest why he wouldn't say the name Jesus.

"You knew what name He came in," she said.

"I didn't want to trap myself," Forest said.

Forest was trapped in his religion and died in the trap.

Daddy, Mother, Juanita, and Arlo were baptized that afternoon in the precious, lovely name of Jesus. They were set free.

# Jesus Came to our House

Mother had been baptized nearly a week. We were Sabbath keepers. We were honest in doing all we knew to do. A neighbor came over and said he was out of water. He had cows, pigs, horses, chickens, and a lot of kids. In all, they had 13 boys and one girl.

"What do I do?" Daddy asked Mother.

"If your ox falls into a pit on the Sabbath day, will you not pull it out?" Mother asked. "The man has to have water."

Daddy went to help. Mother went to the piano, got an old hymn book, and started playing. The children gathered around the piano, except Arlo who stayed in the bedroom. Mother played the song, "I Want to Love Him More." She started playing faster and faster. She played it so fast that her fingers couldn't keep up with her heart. Sterling, 11, me, 9, Bennie, 6, and Hazel, 4, could hardly keep up. Suddenly, she stopped.

"You children run out to play," she said. "I want to read my Bible."

We went. She got on her bed and read. After a few minutes (still at unrest), she laid back on her pillow. She saw a funnel of light from heaven. She thought it was the Holy Ghost. She shouted "Hallelujah" a time or two and started speaking in tongues. I was playing with the rest of the children and wanted a drink of water. I ran to the house to get it. When I heard her speaking in tongues, I ran back to the play yard.

“Mother is getting the Holy Ghost!” I shouted.

We all ran back to the house, and slipped in as if we were entering church while preaching was going on. We got kitchen chairs and lined them up along the bed in neat order. We sat, listened, and waited. I was so hungry for it, but I thought I had to wait. I didn’t know. It seemed to me she spoke in tongues for about an hour.

She was so surprised when she opened her eyes. She didn’t know we were there the whole time.

Did I get my drink of water I went after? I don’t know.

# We Will All Be Right Here

Juanita was just 18 when she married. A week later, she was baptized in Jesus' name on a Saturday night. The following Wednesday, she went to the altar seeking the Holy Ghost.

"Now you pray as long as you want," a young man told her. "We'll all be right here, praying with you "

It was almost 8:30 p.m. when Juanita knelt at the altar, raised her hands, and started praising God. About midnight, Mother slipped Juanita's shoes off. If anyone tried to touch her, or hold her hands up for her, she would lean away from them. People began getting restless at about 1 a.m. Juanita was still holding up her hands and moving her lips as if she was talking to someone, but with no sound. The same young man who said, "We'll be right here," spoke again. "I have to work today." He left. At about 2 a.m., more left. The room had been full of people but family after family left.

At 6 a.m., Juanita let her arms down and opened her eyes. "Where is everyone?" The only people remaining were her husband, his mother, her parents, brothers, and sisters. That was all.

"They all said they would stay," she said in a hurt voice. "It hasn't been long, has it? I was with Jesus."

God wasn't testing her. He tested the ones who declared they would "be right here." They failed that test.

# Determination

Robert and Juanita were a year and a half apart and were always close. Juanita got in church first. She was married. Robert had been baptized and knew he needed the Holy Ghost.

He stopped to see Juanita and told her that he was hungry for the Holy Ghost. She had an old pump organ, but she couldn't play well. Robert said, "play that organ while I pray." She tried several different songs, stopping between each one. She didn't know how.

Finally, in desperation, he jumped up from praying. He took her by the shoulders, shook her and said, "Keep that music going!"

He went back to his knees again and got the Holy Ghost while she tried to play that old pump organ with all her might.

I wish we could find someone today with that kind of hungry determination.

# My Miracle (Only for Me)

The first time I ever realized God did something especially for me was Sept. 23, 1939. I was nine, starting to walk into the cold river water close to Winamac, Indiana.

I was to be baptized in the precious name of Jesus that I might be saved. My first step into the water felt like ice.

"Now, don't think of the cold water," Pastor Duncan said. "Think of what Jesus has done for you."

Immediately, the water felt warm.

# Nosebleed

Robert was accustomed to having nose bleeds. He didn't think much about it. He was at his father-in-law's (Wesley Stephenson) home when it started.

"I can stop that blood by reading Ezekiel 16:6," Wes said.

He hurried and found the scripture, read it to Robert and it bled harder. Wes read it again. Still, it bled harder. He was reading a third time when Robert interrupted.

"Stop it," Robert said. "That's witchcraft."

Wes stopped and so did the blood.

"It takes Jesus to stop the blood," Robert said.

As far as I know, Robert never had another nosebleed.

I saw it tried another time on Sis. McColskey's mother. She had cancer on her nose. The scab came off and it started bleeding. Bro. Robert McColskey read the scripture and it did no good. We prayed and it stopped.

Jesus is our help in time of any trouble.

# CHAPTER 3
## The 1940s

# Allen

We started going to church in house meetings in the middle of July 1939. Mother got the Holy ghost about August 23, and then had a beautiful healthy looking baby boy named Allen Lee on May 21, 1940. Mother turned 45 three months later.

When Mother was still in bed after the birth, (those days they didn't get up until the tenth day), she said an angel whispered to her and asked, "Are you ready?"

"Yes," she said. "But what about my children?"

"I'll leave you and take one of them," the angel said.

Mother said she knew one of her children would die. Which one? She had 10 living. Hazel was always getting hurt. Ava was always sick. Most of them were saved. Ben and Hazel didn't yet have the Holy Ghost, but Hazel wasn't quite five and Bennie only seven. She told only Daddy about the angel.

"Have your own way, Lord," Mother said.

We were having service at our house one Saturday night when Allen was 11 days old and the picture of health. Everyone, of course, wanted to hold and see the baby. To me, he was beautiful. Mother thought the baby didn't seem right. He was breathing okay. His heart was beating even, but she thought something was wrong. She took him in the bedroom, fed him and he went to sleep. After everyone left church, Mother called the doctor.

"How did you know something was wrong?" the doctor asked. "Have you given him anything besides mother's milk? When did you think something was wrong?"

He asked question after question and said he couldn't find anything wrong. But Mother knew something wasn't right.

"Doc, heart trouble runs bad in the family," Mother said.

"I've checked that," the doctor said. "It was fine. But I'll check it again."

At 2 a.m., the doctor discovered blood slowly seeping through a valve that was supposed to close at birth. He said Allen had leakage of the heart and there was nothing that could be done about it.

Over 18 years later, at Bass Lake Church, there was a girl there about 16. She was a flirt with every boy.

"I'm so glad Jesus took Allen home," Mother said. "Allen probably would have picked that flirt for a wife."

Thank you, God!

# Thou Shalt Not Kill

Bro. Dave Losh told a bunch of us Norrises that he believed it was wrong to kill anything for any purpose other than food. He said it is not right to take the life of rats, mice, snakes, bears, bees, opossums, racoons, lions, and other animals unless you killed them to eat. He said God gave us no right to shed blood.

Robert spoke up and pointed out that Bro. Dave killed a mosquito.

"Well, it bit me," Bro. Dave said.

"Oh, you believe in vengeance?" Robert asked.

"…Vengeance is mine saith the Lord." (Romans 12:19)

# Dancing in the Light

My daddy was very shy when he received the Holy Ghost. He never wanted to be noticed.

Daddy started dancing when the spirit of God was strong one night. Different thoughts came to his mind.

"I'm a heavy man. What if I step on someone's feet?"

With his eyes closed, he focused on the light from a kerosene lamp in the center of the room. He could see the brightness through closed eyelids and began to enjoy himself in the spirit as his face glowed in the light.

He danced out of the room, through the dining room and kitchen, into the utility room, and back in the darkest corner. The dancing spirit left him.

The service was all the way at the other end of the house. He didn't know he had left. His eyes had still been on the light.

Jesus is the Light.

# Francesville Revival

I was 10 years old when we attended a 21-day revival in Francesville. Several got baptized and received the Holy Ghost.

My sister Mildred was leading testimony service when people suddenly got quiet, and the aisle cleared. A large truck tire rolled straight up the aisle and hit the altar bench in front. The tire turned over and went around and around at least eight or nine times before coming to rest.

"Thank you," Mildred said. "Thank you very much. Years ago, they threw tomatoes, rotten eggs, or rocks. Thank you. It's only a tire."

Then the blessings of the Lord really fell.

# You Just Ain’t Got It

Shortly after the Francesville revival, a man came to church in one of our house meetings. Everyone who had made a start to live for God was supposed to testify. I didn’t know the man, but he was sitting close to Bro. Dave.

The man got up to preach, testify or whatever. I don’t know. He marched back and forth waving his arms and preaching, I thought.

“Brother, if you ain’t got what I got,” he shouted. “If you didn’t get it like I got it, or you don’t walk like I walk, or you don’t talk like I talk, then you just ain’t got it.”

He jerked off his suit jacket and threw it on the post of a kitchen chair. He did it so quickly that a pack of cigarettes jumped out of his jacket. Bro. Dave grabbed them and quickly slipped them back in the pocket. Bro Dave saw me watching and said to me, “I didn’t get that kind.”

# Ask to Receive

I slept between my two sisters to keep me warm. I was about three. We kept the bed pulled out from the wall because the roof leaked on the bed when it rained.

One night, I must have been crowded too tight. I rolled over the top of Juanita and fell behind the bed and onto the dirt floor. I cried and complained that my ears hurt.

Mother pulled me from behind the bed and then warmed olive oil to put in my ears. It didn't help. Every night, all winter long, I cried with earaches. I couldn't stand any breeze in my ears. As I grew older, I missed a lot of school because of earaches. I still suffered earaches after I was baptized and received the Holy Ghost.

I was very shy. I wouldn't talk to anyone except my family. The preacher came one day when I was home from school, sitting close to the stove with an earache.

Bro. Dave Losh studied Bible with my parents. I knew he had power with God. I also knew he would not pray for me unless I asked.

"What can I do?" an inward voice asked me. "You better ask."

When Bro. Dave prepared to go, I saw him leave the room, and heard him go up the stairs and out the door. I jumped up and ran after him. He had started the motor. I was nearly too late. He rolled down the window.

"My ears hurt," I told him. "Will you pray for my ears?"

He got out, went into the house, anointed my ears with oil, and prayed a simple prayer. That was over 80 years ago, and I have never had another earache.

But I had to ask.

# Hazel – Age 5

Hazel was five in July 1940. In November, I was sitting in church (house meeting) and noticed Hazel at the altar. She was shaking all over and speaking in tongues. Not like anybody else. She spoke so fast.

I wondered if she was too young to get the Holy Ghost. Thoughts kept running through my mind. Is she pretending to get the Holy Ghost? Surely, she wouldn't do that. No one was praying with her. Maybe she doesn't know any better than to pretend. Or maybe it is real. I had the Holy Ghost, but I certainly didn't have any discernment.

I sat and watched her. I was a little ashamed of her because I couldn't believe it was real. I thought she was too young. I have never told this before. After she had proven herself to have the Holy Ghost, I was too ashamed of myself to ever tell my thoughts.

Christmas drew near. At that time, we still got gifts for each other. Mildred, living in Indianapolis, sent us gifts. She sent Hazel a beautiful baby doll in a lovely pink dress. When it arrived, she opened it, and didn't say a word. Mother said, "Don't you like it?" "Yes," she said. "It's ok." But she never seemed one bit enthused at all. She never took it out of the box or played with it. We all wondered why. I sure would have grabbed it if it had been sent to me. It was beautiful.

A few weeks later (right out of the blue), Hazel said, "I bet Mildred didn't know I had the Holy Ghost, or she wouldn't have gotten me that old doll."

Hazel never played with it. She was interested in learning to read so she could read the Bible. She always acted more like an adult than a child.

Oh well, I never quite got to adulthood. I'm only 93.

# Teachers – Daddy and Mother

My daddy spent much of his life traveling by foot, teaching, and spreading God's Word. One very dark night, he was alone. He said there was a light shining from behind him. Several times, when in the mountains, he saw the light showing the way for him to go. Sometimes, he looked back thinking a car was coming.

My mother had her work too. While Daddy was away, she kept our home running smoothly. After supper, she took the Bible, starting at the first, reading and explaining as best she knew. She was learning, too. Sterling, Hazel, and I had the Holy Ghost. Ben was supposed to be seeking.

We all needed teaching. Mother didn't have time to read it all, but she read and taught us. She skipped Numbers and repeats of Chronicles. I loved Mother's Bible reading and teaching. I don't know how she learned so fast unless she was learning as she taught us. I got more Bible teaching from Mother than from any other person in my life. If she didn't know or understand something, she asked Daddy on his return.

I had wonderful parents. The world's best.

# Calling for Prayer

Robert had been sick for some time and asked Bro. Dave to come and pray for him. Mother, the pastor, and his wife drove to Monticello where Robert was lying on the couch in the living room. Bro. Dave prayed while several gathered and started singing, praying, and just worshiping.

When Mother and the Losh family left, Bro. Dave said he did not understand why Robert wasn't well when they got there. The next day, Robert told Mother that he was feeling better shortly after calling for the pastor.

"I wanted to get up and sing with the rest," Robert said. "But I called him to come 30 miles to pray for me, and I couldn't be all right when he got there. So, I just laid still. I wanted to get up and lead that singing."

Robert was a godsent song leader.

# Robert's Punishment

Robert drifted and wasn't living as close to God as he should. We had a wonderful service during one of our house meetings. Chairs were scattered all through the living room for an altar. Some prayed back through to where they should be. Some just wanted a closer walk with God. Almost everyone was praying.

Mother said the Lord spoke to her and said, "Whip him." With her eyes closed, she started crawling down the row of praying people. She heard someone say, "That's it. Track him down." She thought someone was trying to get away from her. Finally, she caught him, pulled him into her lap and started whipping with open hands.

"Harder!" the voice said.

She tried, but the voice repeated, "harder." She thought she was whipping "Bud" Stevenson.

"Oh! Is his mother ever going to be mad?" she thought.

She doubled up her fists and beat without mercy. All with her eyes tight shut. When it was over, she opened her eyes. Behold, Robert, her own married son, lay in her lap exhausted.

After church, someone asked Robert if he knew who was whipping him. He said yes and knew why he got the whipping.

"Well, did it hurt?" someone asked.

"You better believe it hurt," Robert said. "It's the only whipping I ever got from my mother in my life that hurt."

Why didn't he get up and get away?

"I was powerless to move," Robert said. "I had to take my whipping."

After the service, people told Mother the words she heard were never spoken. Lots of people said that was not of God.

But you could never make Robert or Mother believe that. They knew.

# Be Careful What You Pray

We had a big German shepherd dog named Fanny. She minded well and looked after us all. If Mother went anywhere, we brought Fanny inside. Two words sprang the dog into action if spoken with authority. "Get out!" It meant just that! Be it dog, cat, chicken, horse, cow, snake, or person. It got out or Fanny put it out.

When anyone in the family went out to work or play, Fanny went with them and cared for them. One day, the dog followed Arlo and Sterling when they went to cut wood. Fanny ran under a falling tree and was killed. All of us cried. She was part of the family.

News got around about Fanny's death. Bro. Spurlock celebrated and declared that his prayers were answered. He was afraid of that dog.

"That really hurts to think someone would pray the protection of my family be taken away," Mother said.

With Daddy always gone teaching Bible so much, Mother thought we needed the protection that Fanny gave us.

But God was always there.

# The Broken Toe

A horse stepped on Mother's foot and broke her little toe. She tried to cripple around and work.

Saturday night was communion service. I was about 12 and filled with the Holy Ghost and living right. I was washing Mother's feet and forgot about her toe. She jumped when I touched it. I cried.

I prayed as I washed her feet. Suddenly, she jumped up and started shouting, spilling water, and dancing.

"I'm healed! I'm healed!" she said.

I don't think I ever told Mother I was praying for her. I wanted God to have all the glory.

# Not Ready

We were having a good prayer service at the end of a very good house meeting.

"We need to all pray," Daddy said. "Someone here is not ready to go if Jesus came tonight. Jesus is calling. Everyone pray again."

I examined myself. "Lord, don't let me fail," I said.

After everyone went home, Daddy told us again that someone was not ready to go. The next day, a man came to talk. Daddy was at work.

"Sister Norris, do you know who Bro. Norris was talking about last night?" he asked Mother.

"No, Woody," Mother said. "And he doesn't know."

"It was me," he said. "It's a girl. She won't come to church with me, and I can't give her up. I love her too much."

He never came back. He married her and they had a baby. She divorced him and took the baby. He had nothing. He gave up God for nothing.

# Dead Arise

Bro. Dave Losh, the same brother who prayed for my ears, worked at the state park in Winamac, Indiana. Crede Rose, Arlo's father-in-law, also worked there.

Crede was allergic to bee stings and was stung by one while working. He passed out. They carried him into one of the buildings at the park and tried to revive him, to no avail. Finally, he died. They covered him and called the undertaker to come and get him (not quite like it is today).

Before the undertaker came, Bro. Dave went in, shut the door, and prayed for him. He came out and said, "Don't worry, boys. Crede will be all right." They laughed at him to scorn. How can a dead man be all right? In about 10 minutes, Crede came walking out.

"Crede, you were stung by a bee and died," Bro. Dave said. "You know what it takes to be saved. This was your last chance. Another bee will sting you, and I won't be here to pray for you."

About three weeks later, we buried Crede from another bee sting.

# Hazel's Cold Dip

Hazel was in the first grade. We were all walking home from school with Paul Cleghorn, Mary and Annabell Ray, and Joe and Jean Malia. It was probably about 35 degrees with snow on the ground.

Doug Button came around a corner on his big new John Deere tractor and headed straight for Hazel. She jumped in the ditch of icy water and the tractor went on. Had she not jumped, I think Doug would have hit her.

Sterling urged us to get Hazel home quickly for fear she'd get pneumonia. He gave the lunch buckets to Ben, told me to take Hazel's hand and run. He took the other hand, and we ran the half mile. We told Daddy what happened, prompting him to jump in the car and go find the man on the tractor. Hazel was his baby.

Daddy went to the Buttons' home. Doug admitted to doing it. He said Joe hit the tractor with a rock.

"I thought Hazel was his sister, Jean," Doug said.,

"If Joe hit the tractor with a rock, why did you want to pick on his little sister?" Daddy asked. "She didn't do anything."

If that would've happened two years before, Daddy would probably have mopped the ground with Doug. But Jesus came to our house and cooled his temper.

# Sleep Walking

When Daddy walked places to teach the Bible, he liked to take someone with him. One day he took Robert. It was a very dark night. Robert had a flashlight, but only used it when it was very necessary because of the batteries.

They navigated by the feel of the road under their feet. One night, they were both weary and both went to sleep walking.

Suddenly, Daddy threw his arm in front of Robert and yelled, "Stop!" They heard water running below them. Robert pulled out his flashlight. One more step and they would have gone about 30 feet down into the river.

They were awakened one step from death.

I believe God enjoys surprising us with His miracles!

# Saturday Night Beer Cans

From the time we got in church in August 1939 until Jan. 1960, we hosted church on Saturday nights in our home. Then we moved to Arkansas. The Reign family hosted church on Mondays, the John Wesley Stephenson family on Tuesdays, and John Edker Stevenson family on Wednesdays. The Loshes later picked up Thursdays. I don't remember who had Friday services.

We were free on Sunday to go a distance if we could get tires and gas money. We loved to go to Bro. Vaught's in Lafayette, but that was 50 miles.

One Saturday night, someone threw out about 25 beer cans in the entrance of our driveway. Mother picked them up. The same thing happened the following Saturday. Mother again picked them up. This went on for several weeks before Daddy gave us an order.

"Don't pick up the beer cans anymore," Daddy said. "It isn't a good witness to have beer cans in our trash."

The cans were soon run over and buried in the dirt.

The mysterious litterbugs didn't go to the trouble of throwing out anymore.

# One Fast Ride

My Daddy found salvation at age 48. He and Mother had been searching for years but couldn't feel any place was right. The right place was pointed out to them by a foul-mouthed, cigarette-smoking drunkard that worked on the road with him. God can use anything or anybody. In 2 Chronicles 18:20-22, God told a lying spirit to go and entice the king.

It seems that we didn't have a car most of the time. Daddy traveled by foot. The family stayed home before we found God and a lot of the time afterward.

When Daddy went places after he got salvation, he still went afoot to leave the car for church. He said he could talk to more people that way. On one occasion, he said God wanted him to go to Kingsport, Tennessee. He started walking and praying. He had no money or food, but he knew God would take care of him. A couple days passed on his trek, and he still had a long way to go. Then, the Lord spoke.

"You'll be in Kingsport tonight," the Lord told Daddy.

Daddy began to doubt a little as the sun set. Was he sure God spoke? He still had over 100 miles to go.

A pickup truck slid to a stop.

"Hi, stranger," the driver said. "Going far?"

"I'm making my way to Kingsport," Daddy wearily answered.

"Get in the back," the driver said. "That's where I'm going."

Daddy said he never had such a ride (and he had ridden with Robert). He slid from one side of the truck bed to the other as they went around mountains. But he wasn't scared or worried. He knew he would be in Kingsport that night.

And he was.

# Another Mystery

Jimmy and Robert were both stationed in Germany during World War II. Elroy enlisted, dropped the name Elroy, and became Jimmy.

Robert had a wife who was expecting. He could only see with one eye. He was classified 4F, but because of a shortage of men, he was reclassified as 1A and they took him.

Juanita had three small children and a husband who wouldn't support them. One day when she got the mail, there was a strange-looking letter mailed to her with the proper address. She didn't know anyone in Germany. She opened it.

"We are very poor," the writer penned. "We have 4 children. We are hungry. A soldier in the US Army gave me this address and said you would help."

Juanita gave the letter to Daddy. She had nothing to feed her own family. We answered and sent clothing and food several times. We kept in contact for years.

When Jimmy and Robert came home from the service, they both said they didn't give the address to anyone. Why would they? They knew Juanita's situation.

I always believed God knew that family needed help and He helped them.

# Pet Unloaded

Mildred boarded with the Whittens in Indianapolis. Their children, Dora Jean, and Paul Samuel, wanted to go to the farm with Mildred and see what country life was like.

Dora Jean was about the age and size of Hazel, about 10. The girls were both on Pet, the big mare. Usually very safe (Psalm 33:17). She was just standing and suddenly bucked them off and kept standing. Dora Jean was hardly hurt, but Hazel turned solid black from her waist to her knees because of landing so hard on the ground.

Mother and Mildred were inside the house when it happened. Someone told David (about five years old) to run to the house and get Mother and Mildred. He leisurely went in and said calmly, "Pet unloaded."

"What do you mean Pet unloaded?" Mother asked.

"Well, Dora Jean and Aunt Hazel fell off the horse," David said.

When they got up and walked, Mildred called Dora Jean's mother. She said, "Don't worry about it. Just be thankful no bones are broken."

The girls were not seriously hurt. God took care of them.

# Headed Back Home

Dora Jean and Paul Samuel experienced more farm life while visiting. We had a grape arbor and canned lots of juice. Mother bottled it in small bottles. We kept it in the well pit, a bricked-up hole where the well was drilled just outside the house. From there, the water was piped into the basement. The pit kept the drinks cool in summer and freezing in the winter. Paul Samuel loved it. Before he left, Mother told Paul Samuel to take as many bottles of grape juice as he wanted.

The next morning, they were headed home by Greyhound bus.

"Paul Samuel, wake up," Mildred said as she washed his face in cool water. "Paul Samuel, you've got to get up."

She set him up. He was too heavy for her to carry to the car. "Paul Samuel, honey, you've got to wake up. We're going to miss the bus."

He opened one eye slightly and said, "Both of us?"

Daddy had been waiting in the car. He came in and saw the problem, picked up Paul Samuel and loaded him as the rest of the luggage.

They were off to the city.

# Juanita's Trance and Death

Juanita had three children. David was three, Dorothy two and Delores six months. It was church night at her house. She was sweeping the floor, getting ready for service.

Delores was in her baby swing. God spoke to Juanita and said, "Pray." Without picking up her dirt, she set the broom aside and fell to her knees.

God told her that He was going to take Juanita "home."

"I'm ready, Lord," Juanita said. "But what about my children?"

"I'll care for them," God said.

It was about 3 p.m. when John, who was backslidden, came home and called the doctor, Mother, and Daddy. Juanita was in a trance all night. At 6 a.m., Juanita opened her eyes.

"God sent me back to raise my children," Juanita said. "When they are grown, God will come for me again and I will go with Him."

From that time on, we could see she had more and more power with God. She had three more children.

"Why am I having more children?" she asked. "I am supposed to get to go home."

Juanita got sick with the Hong Kong flu during preparations for Wanda's wedding in December 1968. They brought Juanita to our house in Arkansas. She lived there about three weeks. Just a few days before her death, she asked me for a drink of water. When I handed it to her, she took it in both her feeble, shaky hands and said, "Thank you, Jesus, for this nice cold drink of water."

In that moment, I realized that I was not as thankful as I should be. If I wanted a drink of water, I drank it, not realizing God (my Maker) was providing it.

I felt so ashamed.

# Pestered by the Devil

I had a fever and was in my bed asleep. I dreamed my brother, Sterling, was sitting by my bed. He had his legs crossed and his elbows on his knee with his chin in his hands, as he so often sat.

The devil opened my bedroom door and came in. He was really dressed up in red and black, but he had horns about five inches long. He had a chain. He stepped onto my bed, dragging the chain. In my dream, I wondered why Sterling didn't do something to help me. The devil walked around me and stepped over me but didn't touch me. I could feel the chain he dragged.

Finally, I got mad and yelled at the devil.

"Get out of my room!" I demanded.

He stepped off my bed and very slowly left my room. I had taken authority over him.

I woke up and Sterling wasn't there. I was so mad. I sat there in bed. Why didn't I say, "In Jesus name?" Then it came to me. I have His spirit. He gave me power to command satan to leave because "I am" in his name. Thank you, Jesus.

I still prefer to say, "In Jesus name."

# Singing in Tongues

After Jimmy came home from the Army, he went to Wisner, Louisiana. He got a job in Winnsboro and married a backslidden girl. With Robert's help, they started attending church in Jiggers.

We all went to see them. While in church one day, Daddy was asked to sing. Jimmy followed as Daddy walked to the front. Jimmy sat down on the front pew. When Daddy started singing, Jimmy did too. Jimmy didn't know the song as Daddy had written it. But Jimmy carried the tune right along with Daddy. Only Jimmy sang in tongues. It was beautiful and blended so well.

Jimmy said he knew he had to sing with Daddy.

The Lord moves in mysterious ways.

# God Provided Food

Juanita and her children were hungry. One morning, when she got up, she had nothing to feed the children. No bread, milk, meat, or vegetables. Nothing but a little self-rising flour and water. It was Monday morning, and she had just enough to make flour and water pancakes for one breakfast. She couldn't even hope for a few groceries until Friday evening.

She decided to use half of the pancake mixture. That would give each of the four children one pancake. The next morning, she did the same thing. The flour and the grease to fry them lasted the week.

God had intervened.

# Back to the Barstool

There was a young girl, raised in church, but spoiled. She got everything she wanted that wasn't sinful. She left home as soon as she could, went into the world, and married a worldly man,

She and her husband were sitting on barstools one night. She said the Lord spoke to her and said, "You don't belong here." She shrugged it off and went on drinking.

She started screaming one night. Her husband couldn't help her. He took her in his arms until he could calm her. The Lord had been shaking her over hell's hot flames.

She told him all about how she left her parents and the church for the world. They called her pastor around 1 a.m. Bro. Petty and his wife prayed them both through to the Holy Ghost. The husband was baptized that night and they went on their way rejoicing.

A couple months later, they were dabbling with the world. Within a year, they were back on the barstool.

# Andrew Fields

Daddy baptized Andrew Fields, a young man who had been in and out of church. We knew and loved him,

Andrew, a widower, went to Kentucky and found a widow woman named Daisy. She thought he needed to be baptized again. After the baptism and marriage, Andrew spoke to his father-in-law about his baptism.

"I've been baptized five times," Andrew said.

"Next time, get baptized in tar," his father-in-law said. "Maybe it will stick tighter."

# My Little Susie

Daddy heard of a woman from Francesville named Thelma who wanted to go to church. Daddy found her husband, Leonard, and asked if Thelma and their children could go.

We stopped and picked them up Wednesday night on our way to church. When we got to church, Daddy asked me to take the children in while they talked to Thelma.

Thelma told them her life. She was raised in a religious home, but not Apostolic. She had happily married. After her son Dicky was born, her husband left her for another. She said that she lost her mind.

A sailor then came into her life. When he found out she was expecting Susie, he went back to camp. She tried to trace him. There was no one in camp by that name he gave her. Not in the navy or anywhere.

"I was raised better than that," Thelma told my folks.

Daddy laid out the plan of salvation to Thelma. She was baptized that night and received the Holy Ghost a few days later.

Little Susie became very dear to me. She is now 76, lives in Midway, Arkansas, has four children, three grandchildren and one great granddaughter. She lives for Jesus with all her heart.

# What You Eat All that Bread For?

Life was serving Juanita's family a little better. The children had gone hungry most of their lives. Daddy made a deal with a big grocery store in Monticello to get all the outdated bakery things (breads, rolls, pies, cakes, donuts, etc.). We picked it up twice a week. After picking up the food, we drove by Juanita's home and let her get what she wanted.

We hadn't been doing it long when one day Juanita's family sat down for lunch. They feasted on peanut butter sandwiches. Delores, about five at the time, started to get herself another slice of bread, looked, pulled back her hand and sat back.

"Honey, why didn't you get yourself a slice of bread when started to?" her mother Juanita asked. "I saw you start to get some."

"Noooooo," Delores said as she shook her head slowly. "Daddy would say 'ya ya ya ya. What you eat all that bread for?'"

God sees every sparrow that falls. What will He do with a man who doesn't provide for a mother, children, and babies?

God has all the answers.

# Dorothy's Burn

Juanita's oldest daughter Dorothy was about seven when she suffered a burn from ironing clothes. The iron turned over on her leg, making a burn about the length of the iron. Juanita, as usual, started to pray.

"No! Don't pray," Dorothy said. "I don't want you to."

Juanita secretly prayed.

"Why Lord?" Juanita asked. "What has gone wrong? Why doesn't she want prayer?"

Juanita applied burn salve and a bandage. The next day, it was worse. Dorothy still refused prayer, even though burn streaks were running from the burn site. Bloody infection oozed down her leg a week later. Juanita didn't know what to do when she started to dress it. It was then Dorothy started to cry.

"Mommy, pray for my leg," Dorothy pleaded.

Her leg was healed two days after her request for prayer.

# Butch

It was the spring of 1949. We lived in Northern Indiana and had close black friends, the Fred Wills family, who lived 50 miles away in Lafayette. The color of skin made no difference to me.

Daddy and Bro. Wills sat for hours searching the scriptures. Bro. Wills wanted Daddy to help him spread the gospel to his family in Brownsville, Tennessee. Hazel and I went with Daddy. Some others decided to go in a separate car. All went well for about two days.

The driver of the other car asked that Hazel and I go home with them in his carload that night. I told him I came with my daddy and Bro. Wills, and I would go back the same way. I was 19 and Hazel 13. The driver told me there was going to be bad trouble and he didn't want us in it. That carload left for home that evening. I don't know if it was before or after church.

The service was great, but Daddy saw the devil with smoke coming from the back of his shirt collar.

"The devil is really mad," Daddy said.

The next day, Daddy and Bro. Wills went to town. Hazel and I went for a walk down the old, dusty mountainside. It was beautiful. I liked it there. We were happy. God is good. We started back and a police car stopped beside us.

"What are you girls doing here?" the policeman asked.

I told him that we were visiting and pointed to the house where we were staying.

"That's what I thought," the policeman said. "Get in the backseat. I heard you were here."

We obeyed. Hazel and I hung tight together. The police stopped at the house. One officer stood guard at the car while the other went to the house. Sis Wills stepped out on the porch. I couldn't hear what he or she said. But the officer slapped her on the side of the face so hard he nearly knocked her down. They talked a bit and the policeman got back in and drove us to the police station.

"Get out!" he ordered.

They took us in the station and told us where to sit. They left to hunt for Daddy and Bro. Wills. They happened to be parked close to the station studying the Bible. They were ordered out of the car and searched. Daddy kept his Bible in his hand with his fingers in the place they were reading. The officers ordered them to go inside the building.

"Look at him toting that Bible," one officer said. "Somebody ought to kill him."

The officers tried to start a riot, but God had his hand on us. They first questioned Bro. Wills.

"Where were you born? When did you move to Indiana? When did you come back in town? Why? Do you know any white people here? Who?"

Mr. Wills told the police the name of the white man he knew in town. The police found the man and took him to the station.

When the man saw Mr. Wills, he cried out.

"Butch! Where have you been?" he asked. "I've missed you." He gave him his hand and patted him on the back.

"Yes, I know him," the man told the police. "But it's been a long time."

The officer turned to Daddy.

"Do you know what I would do if I was you?" the officer asked. "I'd pick up these two daughters and get out of town as fast as I could."

Daddy stood, motioned to us, and stopped.

"Sir, I have no car and no money," he said. "I came with Fred Wills."

"Then get in the car with that [racial slur] and go and don't come back," the racist officer said.

God takes care of His own but how did the other "brother" know there was going to be bad trouble? And why did he come to me instead of Daddy and Bro. Wills?

# Thorns

Did you ever go blackberry picking
And find that the biggest and best
are those far deep in the briars?
Oh! They're much bigger than all the rest.
So you wade through the thickest of jungle
You will have the best of the lot
The thorns and the scratches won't matter
Just look at the berries you've got.

Now the rose is another example.
Its beauty is rare to behold,
And the sweet perfume from its beauty
Is something that never grows old.
I will have the biggest and nicest
To put in a vase or to wear
Oh, the scratches we must endure
of those we don't have a care.

Now there are other thorns in this life
As we tread this worrisome way.
These thorns are placed by the devil
To cause us to go astray
But the best is not far away
Those the thorns and the brambles are there
With our eyes on the goal, we can make it
And Heaven, with Jesus we'll share.

# CHAPTER 4

## The 1950s

# Marvin

Juanita's youngest son, Marvin, loved to mow grass. We had an old mower like they had when I was born. It was good and we tried to keep the grass mowed between the garage and the house to keep the sand burrs down.

Marvin mowed every time he went to Grandma's house. Mother was afraid he would get hurt. The mower was sharp. One day he got a corn cob caught in it. He pulled the cob out with his hand. That released the tension. The blade turned and almost cut off the end of his finger.

"That's it!" Mother said. "No more mowing."

They took him to the doctor to get it sewed up. Marvin still cried. Dr Hallack put him on the table.

"Marvin, does it really hurt that bad?" the doctor asked.

"No, but I like to mow," Marvin said.

"Of course, you do," the doctor responded. "And Grandma isn't going to stop you. You won't do it again will you?"

Marvin promised he wouldn't.

"You heard that, Grandma," the doctor said. "That boy needs to mow the lawn and you need to let him."

We lived in Indiana. Juanita took her family of six children and moved to Louisiana. Marvin mowed every chance he got.

When he was about 8, he cut his foot while mowing a neighbor's yard. He sat down on the neighbor's front steps to watch it. Every time his heart beat, the blood shot. A neighbor boy that Marvin often played with came by and took one look.

"Boy, you is bleeding to death," his friend said.

The boy jerked off his shirt, ripped some strips of it, made a tourniquet, wrapped it tightly around Marvin's ankle, threw Marvin over his own shoulder and carried him home.

He was a real friend.

# David's Shirt

My mother's mother and brothers lived about 300 miles away in Illinois. Juanita hadn't seen them in years and wanted to visit them. We had an old car, but the tires were bad. I could stop on the roadside, patch a tire, pump it up, and on the road again.

So, we started. I don't know how many flats we had, but that one. But that one! And about 50 miles to go yet. The tire was worn. I could patch the tube, but I couldn't run on a tube.

Mother told me about a time that Daddy had a tire like that. He used a folded diaper to cover the hole. And he made it home. But we didn't have a baby, so we didn't have a diaper.

Juanita ripped the back out of David's shirt and handed it to me. David was nine at the time. I patched the tube, folded the back of the shirt, placed it over the hole, put the tube in and pumped it up. We ran it that way for about three months.

God always makes a way for His own.

# A Bad Burn

It was about 1953. Mother cooked on an old wood cookstove. I had an old 1936 Chevy pickup.

We decided to get a load of kindling from the cabinet factory dump. Mother needed it. I took my truck for kindling. Juanita and the kids took Ben's car. We had permission to get kindling any time. When we got there, it had been set afire the night before as they often did. There was still plenty. Marvin (about 5) was playing around while we loaded.

Soon we heard a scream. There was Marvin with his knees on a bucket, barefoot and hot embers all around him. Someone with heavy shoes got him off the bucket. Marvin stepped on the bucket to get some sticks he wanted. The bucket turned over and dumped him in the embers. His feet and ankles were both severely burned.

We all got into the car and headed to the Joneses who lived in town. Sis. Jones said to put his feet in ice water with aspirin to stop the pain, but she had no aspirin. I rushed to the drugstore to get aspirin, burn salve and bandages. I ran into the store, ran back to the car, and headed back to the Joneses. Whoops! A red light behind me. What now? I wasn't speeding. I stopped. Why was he stopping me? I'm in a hurry. Marvin is hurting.

The officer came to the car.

"Lady, you seem to be in an awful hurry," he said.

"I am," I said. "My little nephew just got badly burned. They sent me to the drugstore. Can you follow me? I'm going to the Joneses home."

"I'm sorry I stopped you," he said. "I know where they live. Follow me."

He hurried to his car, kept his light flashing, and drove to the Joneses' home. He said I need not check you.

We worked with Marvin for about 10 or 15 minutes. He was still crying hard with pain.

Suddenly, Juanita ordered us to take Marvin's feet out of the water and wrap them in a dry towel. We did as his mother asked. She laid her hand on the towel on his feet and bowed her head. He quit crying loudly and settled down to not crying at all in just a few minutes. The next day, he was up walking on those burnt feet.

The police never knew that my purse, driver's license, and everything else was in my truck at the dump. Neither did the thieves.

Ain't God good?

# The Cigar

Years ago, men who fathered babies gave out cigars to their friends. It was a tradition, even if neither of them smoked.

Nita Fahlgren was a young girl, about 13. The family was not in church yet. Some new father gave John a cigar.

"Mom, I'm going to smoke it," Nita said.

"Nita, I said no!" Hazel said. "But if you are determined to do it, then you are going to sit right down there and smoke it all!"

Nita laughed and lit up. When it was about a third gone, Nita said, "Mom, I can't do it."

"You will," Hazel said. "You won't get up until you do."

All the fun was gone. Nita was sick. She sucked in and blew out, trying not to inhale any more than necessary.

Nita's mother was firm.

"You chose it," she said. "Now you do it."

The outcome was an extremely sick girl who never wanted anything to do with smoke for the rest of her life.

When she was grown, she was ashamed.

# Teenage Driving

My daddy drove like a teenager. He thought 65 miles per hour was the going speed on a two-track, one-lane gravel road. He was an excellent driver, but he loved speed.

Daddy and my 4-year-old son, Charles, were going somewhere. Harvy Crawford pulled out of his driveway and did not see the fast approaching "racecar," so he plowed right into the side of Daddy's car. It was summer, before any thought of air conditioning or seatbelts. All four windows were down.

It didn't take much to flip Daddy's car on its top when it was almost airborne already. As soon as the car stopped sliding on its top, Charles was out of it like a jackrabbit out of a hole. It took a little longer to get a 220-pound man out since the doors didn't want to open with it on its top.

Neither one got a scratch. Daddy got a small particle of glass in his eye. Someone saw the car sitting in front of our garage and said, "It's certain nobody came out of that car alive." They were wrong.

Just another piece of God's handiwork.

# Tornado

I was working for some people near Lafayette, Indiana. They had two children. The parents had been baptized but didn't have the Holy Ghost. They were very faithful to church. The two children and I slept upstairs.

The storm began. I wanted to really pray and call out loudly to God, but I was not sure of myself or my surroundings. I slipped down the stairs and out the front door. The wind whipped me from all sides. I ran to the garage which is not the best place to weather the storm. I got in the car and cried out for God to spare the family who was seeking and needing Him. When the storm passed over, they came hunting me.

Across the road, the neighbors had a row of beautiful large trees. The owner said he bought the home because he loved those trees. They were ruined. It was a rent house. The roof of the house fell on the little girl's bed upstairs. The little boy who slept downstairs had gone to visit his grandmother that night, so they let the little girl sleep in his bed.

Coincidence? Or God?

Our house was next. The tornado lifted over our house, dropping one small limb on the kitchen roof. The storm stayed up until it passed the outbuildings and a large barn. The tornado dropped down again and flattened trees for over a mile, and about a quarter-mile wide.

People said my prayers kept everyone safe. I say it was God's handiwork. I didn't pray for the little boy to visit his grandmother so the little girl could sleep downstairs.

If I had anything to do with it, it was only obedience to God. He woke me and gave me a mind to pray.

To God be the glory!

# Attempted Kidnapping

We had just built a house on the top of the basement in which we lived for about 20 years. The upstairs wasn't finished yet, but we were sleeping upstairs. The bottom of the basement windows was just above ground level. There was a small snake trying to get in the window. We asked Daddy to go kill it. He didn't seem to be much concerned.

"It's only a small snake," Daddy said. "Nothing compared to the size of the two-legged snake that will be trying to get in here."

He had already told us someone was trying to kidnap Charles. Not because they wanted him but because they didn't want me to have him. From the time he was born, we had to guard him. Daddy saw a vision of Charles thrown in the Big Sandy River in Pikeville, Kentucky.

We told Charles to never go downstairs at night by himself. At that time, the only bathroom was downstairs. Daddy never turned on a light when he went downstairs, but Charles turned on every light as he followed Daddy. As Charles walked through the kitchen, he heard a noise behind him. He saw a man he didn't know. Charles turned and ran in the bathroom. Daddy started to reprimand him for coming in when Charles interrupted.

"Grandpa, there's a man in there," Charles said.

Daddy took him by the hand and started back. They checked the two outer doors on the ground level as they went up. Both closed. There were no locks on the doors at that time.

They came up and woke us. We all got up to search the house. As we all went back downstairs, we noticed the outside door was open a crack. The man hid under the steps in the storage room and went out as soon as Daddy and Charles went up.

I have really learned in having the Holy Ghost 83 years that God is always there standing between us and the devil. He knows the devil's tricks and can keep and protect us if we only faithfully trust Him.

Jesus, I praise and trust You!

# Beverly

I had a Sunday school class of several children ages 4-6. Beverly, the pastor's daughter, was one of them. Cutting hair came up in the lesson. I told them it was wrong to get their hair cut. We read it to them, but one little girl who had unsaved parents and came with her grandmother wanted her hair cut. Grandma said no!

"I used to have beautiful long hair clear down to here," Beverly said as she pointed to her waist. "But my aunt cut it off. I didn't want her to do it."

Beverly's mother had already told me how much her daughter wanted hair but couldn't grow it. It was short and very curly.

The following Sunday, the other little girl came with her long, blond hair all cut off and gone.

"If it's alright for Beverly, then I can do it, too," the girl said.

Her worldly mother cut it.

Beverly realized at age five what her lie had done. Her mother made her tell the class that she wanted long hair, so she pretended that she once had it.

Beverly was later baptized and received the Holy Ghost. She became a dedicated young lady and married a good Christian boy who became a minister.

# Guns

When my son Charles was born, I said "no toy guns!" Every gun is to be treated as a real gun. I taught him that guns are dangerous.

When Charles was four, I was caring for a bedfast woman. I had a birthday at my job for him. He got a necktie from the pastor's family. When he opened it, he said "oh boy, just what I always wanted." But the evangelist bought him twin pistols with holsters. When he opened that gift, his face fell.

"We don't play with guns, do we Mother?' he asked.

"No, honey, we don't," I said.

He later asked what he should do with the guns.

"What do you want to do with them?" I asked.

"Take them out on the hill and bury them."

He took the guns and used his small toy shovel to bury them on the hill where he often played in the sand. It took him about an hour to get the hole just right. Once he covered the holsters and guns, he stomped on the dirt to make sure they were good and buried.

About six years later, Charles wanted me to take him hunting. Mother had an old .410 shotgun. It was winter, but not really cold. A fresh snow had fallen in the night. I had never gone hunting. But since Charles' daddy had left him when he was just a baby (five months), I didn't want to fail him. His grandpa said to look for rabbit tracks in the snow and follow them.

Charles was enthused. I had never shot a gun. My practice had been with a BB gun. I always believed God was helping me be like a father to my son.

Suddenly, there sat a rabbit by a stump. We both saw it about the same time. I shot and grabbed the rabbit, set my foot on its head, and pulled it off. I taught Charles to never eat blood with the meat. We hunted a little longer, but he was satisfied with one rabbit. We skinned and dressed it together. Mother fried it for supper.

He bought his own gun with his own savings. I told him that he must follow the rules and treat all guns as if they are loaded.

His friend from school, Jimmy Pratt, came home with him for the evening. The boys were in his bedroom talking and laughing. They were about 14. I heard a loud boom. Charles' gun had gone off. Not another sound. Daddy, Mother, Hazel, and I all froze. Then we heard them giggle. Charles took his "unloaded" gun, shouted "there's a duck" and shot at duck decals on the cornice board over his windows.

What if we had let him play with toy guns? Would he have shot his friend. I thank Jesus so much.

My brother Jimmy's little grandson didn't make it so well. He was shot and killed at about 12 by the little neighbor boy who thought he had an unloaded gun.

Thank you, Jesus, for being with us. I hate to see children play shoot-and-kill with toy guns and people.

# The Change

Nita Fahlgren was 16 and wasn't in church yet. She had two boyfriends she was dating. She wanted to get rid of both and get right with the Lord.

But how?

She contrived the idea of writing love letters to both. She told the red head how she always loved red hair, that it was beautiful, and how she just couldn't wait to see him again. She told the boy with the black hair how she loved his beautiful and wavy hair. Both letters were full of "love-you-so-much." She stamped and addressed the envelopes, but purposely put each letter in the wrong envelope.

She never heard from the red head again. But the boy with the black hair came to see her.

"Do you happen to know a red headed boy named Bill?" he asked.

She innocently said, "Yes. Why?"

"Oh, I just wanted to know," the boy said.

He never came back.

Nita felt free. She received the Holy Ghost on the way home from youth service. Oh, what a change in her life. That was nearly 65 years ago.

# Billy Boling

Daddy was working in his shop and praying. Frank Boling came to his mind. He was a neighbor when my older siblings were small. Frank was an infidel. You didn't talk God to him. His wife believed in God and taught the children as much as she knew.

Billy, Frank's son, was playing in the yard. A hot electric rod ran down the outside of the garage. Billy grabbed it and stuck fast. Mother heard a commotion outside and saw a man with a stick trying to get Billy loose. Mother ran, thinking she could grab him and break him loose with her speed. She was willing to give her life for the little neighbor boy if it didn't work.

It worked. Little Billy got all right. It was known all over town that Mrs. Norris saved the life of little Billy Boling.

Frank didn't believe in God, so Daddy wanted to talk to him. Daddy hitchhiked, not knowing if the Bolings still lived in the same place. He asked the mail carrier if the Bolings still lived where they used to live years ago. The mail carrier said they moved out of town and then offered to take Daddy to their new address. Mrs. Boling was home. Frank was working.

"Frank is even worse," Mrs. Boling said. "He's harder against God than he used to be."

Daddy tried to talk to Frank, but he was as hard as a nail that hung Jesus to the cross.

Their son was a different story. Mrs. Boling asked for Daddy to talk to Billy who had been studying the Bible and received the Holy Ghost.

"He says he spoke in another language and needs to be baptized in Jesus' name," Mrs. Boling told Daddy. "Stay here tonight and go to Billy in the morning."

Daddy walked 10 miles to Billy's house the next morning. He met Billy in the yard, and they talked. Billy took Daddy in the house to meet his wife.

"Do you remember the woman I told you about that saved my life?" Billy asked his wife. "This is her husband. He's come to save my soul."

He asked Daddy to stay the night.

"I want to pray and be sure you are the one God sent," Billy said.

The next morning, Daddy baptized Billy in his own pond. It reminds me of Phillip and the eunuch.

They all went on rejoicing.

# Just a Small Matter to God

I led the singing and played the accordion at church for about 30 years or more. There was a time I got a bad cold, my tonsils swelled, I could barely talk, and I ran a fever. We lived 25 miles away from church. I wanted to stay home. Mother said she would not leave me alone as sick as I was.

I went to church just like I was. I didn't wash, dress, or comb my hair. I was too sick. I intended to stay in the backseat of the car, but the pastor said no. They helped me to the back seat of the church.

When the service started, the church people all came back to pray for me. Sis. Cora Barnette put her hand on my throat. As she took her hand away, all the pain, swelling, fever and sickness went with it.

I know Sis. Barnett didn't heal my body. God did.

I led singing and played Hazel's accordion that night.

To God, it was a small matter. To me, it was great.

# Big Cat and Little Dog

Juanita, David, and Marvin went to Monroe for something, leaving the girls at home alone. They had a flat while coming back in the middle of the swamps. The spare was also flat and there were no cars on the road that night. They started walking. They walked for some time before hearing a wild cat of some kind. The boys hung tightly to their mother as she hurried along.

They heard it again, but it sounded much closer. It sounded even closer when they heard it a third time. They were in God's hands. There was nothing they could do but hurry and pray.

They passed a house where a little dog barked. And then they heard the cat again. Very loud and very close. Juanita put an arm around each boy and prayed. The little dog yelped. Then not another sound.

"The little dog gave its life to save ours," Juanita said.

Juanita never forgot the little black and white dog.

# Juanita

Juanita did not keep a clean house. Not a filthy house, but a cluttered house. Nothing was ever put where it belonged.

One of the little girls lost her shoes. She hunted the house over.

"Mommy, I can't find my shoes," she said.

"Honey, the last time I wore them, I put them where they belonged," Juanita told her.

"Well, they are still there then because I haven't seen them since," the child said.

# I Guess You'll Have To

A church member who was about 19 or 20, needed a job. Daddy told him he could stay with us for a while and work in the fields until he could do better. He wasn't afraid of work. All went well for a short while. He took a lot of hard work from Mother when he wasn't on the job. He saved his money until he had enough to buy a used car.

We had a small car and needed a larger one to taxi our family, Juanita's family, and the man everywhere. When the man got his car, we were all happy. Hazel, Charles, and I rode to church with him. Daddy picked up Juanita and family.

On the way to church, I noticed decals of women with improper clothing on the back windows of the man's car. I started to scratch them off when I got to church.

"Don't start scratching," he said.

That made me mad.

"I don't like riding in a car with THOSE kinds of pictures," I said.

"Ha, I guess you'll have to," he said.

"And I guess I don't," I shot back.

I went in the church and told Mother. She asked me what I was going to do." I told her that I was going to walk. It was 25 miles. I was 27 and Hazel was 21. We were together. Mother suggested walking to the highway, catching the Greyhound bus and traveling to Mildred's house for about three days.

"Daddy will get rid of him," Mother promised.

So, we did.

The man learned "right" came first with us.

# Falling Window

The Bass Lake Church was an old church. It reminded me of the song "The Little Brown Church," only the church was white. The building was well kept. The windows opened for air conditioning. The bathrooms were two small buildings out back. It sat on a knoll, facing the lake across the road.

The windows seemed to have a mind of their own and closed with a bang. One morning, a little girl was playing in the window with her hands and arms in the windowsill. Hazel, knowing the habit of that window, got up and spoke to the girl's mother.

"Please don't let the baby play in the window," Hazel said. "Sometimes it drops and would hurt her bad."

She gave Hazel a "mind-your-own-business" look. But she took the little girl and sat her down beside her.

Hazel had just sat down behind the mother when the window closed with a bang. A scared look came over the mother's face. Then she smiled at Hazel to show her thankfulness

God is so good to us. We surely can't count His blessings.

The next day, Daddy made wooden props for all the windows.

# The Lord is Coming in July

We were going to Bass Lake Church where many people had been baptized. The altar was full every night. Preaching was good. People seemed hungry. We prayed. Fasted for people to receive the Holy Ghost. But to no avail.

One day, Daddy was working in his welding repair shop. The Lord spoke to him and said He was coming in July. Daddy then rushed into the house.

"I don't understand," Daddy said. "The Bible says no man knoweth the day nor the hour. But God said He was coming in July."

Mother told him not to worry about it.

"If God said it, it's true," she said. "We must just be ready."

During the first service in July, three got the Holy Ghost. Several more received the Holy Ghost that month. Two carloads went to a special service in another town. Three got the Holy Ghost in the car on the way home.

About 40 people got the Holy Ghost in July.

# Nita and the Picture

A picture of Jesus hung in the front of Bass Lake Church. Nita Fahlgren, a young girl who had recently received the Holy Ghost, was dancing in the spirit. I think she was 15. She said God spoke to her and said, "take that picture down." She tried to get it, but others got in her way. Obviously, they knew what she was trying to do.

Finally, she grabbed it and threw it as hard as she could. It sailed over the top of people and landed unharmed in the back of the church. That night, after the picture was down, Sis. Smith got the Holy Ghost. Then she testified.

"I've been seeking God for a long time," Sis. Smith said. "I thought I couldn't pray without being under that picture. As soon as she took it down, I got the Holy Ghost."

She went home and got rid of all these "supposed-to-be" pictures of Jesus. Another sister picked up the "thrown down" picture and put it up in her living room.

# Foot Water -- Gone

It was communion and foot washing night. Service was over, but some were still praising and worshiping God. He was still blessing.

Rebecca, a little girl of about eight, was still dancing. I just happened to see her open one eye and look across the room to the pan of ladies' foot water. I quickly picked up the pan and emptied it before placing it back in the same spot. Rebecca danced on, getting closer and closer to the pan of water. Finally, she touched the rim of the pan with her ankle. Then she sat her foot on the edge of the pan and over it went.

Mother and Juanita looked at me. I smiled. We all knew. Nothing needed to be said.

# Right Comes First

Wanda was in the ninth grade and Marvin was in fourth in Liddieville, LA. Marvin was small and slow for his age because of health reasons. His classroom was sent to P.E. where they had a man teacher.

"All you boys pull off your shirts," the P.E. teacher said.

Marvin didn't talk back or say anything. The teacher told him several times to pull off his shirt. He acted as if he didn't hear. Finally, the teacher sent for "Big Sister" Wanda.

"You need to make Marvin understand that he needs to pull off his shirt for P.E." the teacher said.

"Do what?" Wanda asked. "Pull off his shirt in front all these girls? He better not do such an indecent thing!"

"Well, he will!" the teacher declared. "I'll whip you, you young smartie."

The teacher pulled off his belt.

"You will not lay a hand on me," Wanda said. "I refuse to let any man touch me. My own Daddy never did, and YOU won't be the first one."

He started putting his belt back on, saying all the time he would whip her.

“You will not lay a hand on me,” Wanda repeated. “And Marvin will not take his clothes off in public.”

Wanda and Marvin were both good students. Wanda made high marks which Marvin could not achieve. But they were both liked by their teachers and classmates.

When it came to right and wrong, they couldn’t be swayed.

# Obey Daddy? God? Who?

It was winter. I had been told numerous times to never pick up anyone when we girls were alone. That was drilled in me from the time I started driving.

Hazel and I were going home from New Jersey. We were in Pennsylvania. Snow blew hard on the icy mountain interstate highway where a small soldier walked alone. Daddy said not to pick up anyone, but scriptures came to my mind.

"…If she hath lodged strangers…" (1 Timothy 5:10)

Then other thoughts came to mind.

"Obey your parents. Daddy is head of the house."

I passed that cold, lonely soldier.

Oh, God, forgive me if I made the wrong decision. I couldn't get him off my mind. When I got home, I asked Daddy if I did the right thing.

"Ava, God is your protector," he said. "When you are out, listen to Him first. But be sure it's Him."

I never had that opportunity again. I've passed many walking people, but it wasn't the same. I always felt I failed that time.

But I still don't know.

# Trying the World

Mildred told us about a young couple who wanted to find out what it would be like to live as the world. They were both raised in church. Both received the Holy Ghost at a young age.

They decided to just try the world for one week. They told the pastor what they were going to do.

"The Lord is merciful," they said. "He will forgive us."

The pastor begged them to reconsider, but their minds were made up. During that week, they smoked, drank, and stepped out on each other. They wanted to try all the world had to offer.

The week of carousing ended. When Sunday morning rolled around, they were up as usual and getting ready for church. Now they were coming back to God. So foolish. They left God for seven days of worldly pleasure.

But was it pleasure?

They were both killed in a car wreck on their way back to God and to church.

# Trimming Hair

Several young girls and young married ladies attended Bass Lake Church. Some said it was all right to trim the dead ends from their hair. Some said no. Some said long hair was a glory. But how long was long?

One day, one of the worldliest girls approached Mother.

"Sister Norris, don't you think it would be all right if I just trimmed the dead ends of my hair and evened it up a bit?" she asked.

"Barb, you can look at my hair and my girls' hair and see what I believe," Mother said. "We all have long, untrimmed hair. One look should be enough."

# Look, I'm Doing This for God

Hazel Fahlgren wasn't really interested in church, but she went to please a friend. She was a very happy, friendly person, in pants and hair about two inches long. She came a few times then brought her husband and two children, Dick, 19, and Nita, 15. Dick never attended much but the rest did. They were baptized and received the Holy Ghost.

But Hazel hated long hair.

Getting dressed properly was easy for her. She just couldn't let that hair grow. She knew what the Bible said about it, but she didn't want long hair. But one day her attitude changed.

"See this mop of hair?" Hazel asked. "I don't like it but I'm doing this for God."

In about three years, her hair was thicker and longer than mine ever had been.

Hazel got sick and was admitted to the hospital. She got worse. Her husband went to see her after work every day. One evening, she was in high spirits.

"I'm going home tomorrow," she said.

That was a surprise to her husband, but he was happy. He went home planning to pick up Hazel the next morning.

She went to her heavenly home about 1:30 a.m. A nurse found her already gone. Hazel knew when no one else did.

My best memory of her is holding her beautiful, thick hair that grew longer than the length of her arms and saying, "Look, I'm growing this for God."

# CHAPTER 5
## The 1960s

# Potatoes

Juanita taught her children to trust in God. Wanda especially followed her teaching. The family was leaving for church Sunday morning. As they started away from the door, Wanda stepped back into the house. She got a kitchen chair and firmly set it down, just inside the front door and closed the door.

“Why did you do that?” one of the others asked.

“Because I’m hungry and I expect there to be 10 pounds of potatoes on that chair when I get home from church,” Wanda said.

She marched on to church as a soldier going to war. When they returned home, there wasn’t just 10 pounds but 20 pounds of potatoes sitting on that chair. The older married sister saw them on sale that morning and bought them.

Did that “just happen” or did God answer Wanda before she asked?

# Long Prayers

When Linda came to live with us at age 12, she was already baptized and supposedly had the Holy Ghost.

She was a very good child, but I couldn't see much manifestation of the Holy Ghost. She was attentive in church, and we all prayed together before going to bed. Linda's prayer time was usually very short, but she got on her knees before going to bed.

"Linda sure has a short prayer," Hazel said one night. "She hits the floor with one knee while putting the other in bed."

Linda said, "Oh, Aunt Hazel, it's not that long." She meant to say, "It's longer than that."

Linda left home at 21 and went into the world. She was out of church for 45 years. I was about to give up on her.

Then, in January 2017, she really came to God. Now she is trying to win her two children.

I praise the Lord for my Linda now.

# Tony and Homer

Five-year-old Tony Heims could already play a little on the piano. He was given a 12-bass accordion and was doing great on it. He was learning music and seeking God. One night he got the Holy Ghost.

His grandpa, Homer Caudill, was always telling the church of some dream he had. Homer wasn't there when Tony got the Holy Ghost, but they spoke later.

"Tony, I hear you got the Holy Ghost," Homer said.

"Yes, Grandpa, I did." Tony replied.

"Then let me hear you speak in tongues," Homer said.

"Grandpa, let me see you dream a dream."

# Javonna

Javonna visited her grandparents, Bro. and Sis. Simmons, when she was three. She was playing at the upstairs window.

She unlatched the upstairs window screen and fell about 15 feet to the concrete patio below. They rushed her to the doctor. She wasn't hurt at all! She still has the receipt the doctor gave them. It cost a whole $5.

That was 1963. Now it would be closer to $500.

# No More Peeping Toms

Juanita raised a goat to butcher. She and the children could have butchered it, but a neighbor man wanted to do it for the insides. With David's help, the neighbor said he would cut it up into small enough pieces that Juanita could handle it.

Juanita said she would shoot the goat if the neighbor and David cut its throat. They tied the goat to the fence, inside the goat pen.

"She'll miss it!" the neighbor said. "She's gonna miss that goat! She can't hit that goat."

Boom!

The goat dropped. They cut its throat. Juanita went back in the house with the children.

"Man! She did hit that goat," the neighbor said. "I wouldn't want her getting a bead on me. It's dead. Did you see how fast that goat dropped?"

Prior to the butchering, Juanita had a little trouble with night prowlers, The children saw faces looking in the windows. Never again did the children see anyone peeping in the windows or hear noises at night. The prowlers did not want "her bead" on them.

God has a way of handling a situation if we trust in Him.

# The Broken Foot

Juanita and her family were building a fence for a neighbor. She and her children took any work they could find to support themselves. The children's father had long ago quit paying support. He remarried and supported that family.

Somehow, Juanita broke her foot. The children took her to the house and to bed. Robert helped by bringing over some groceries. Jimmy (Elroy) came to make fun. By that time, the foot was swollen to twice its normal size. Jimmy laughed.

"I guess now you'll go to the doctor!" Jimmy said.

"No, Jimmy," Juanita said. "That foot may kill me, but I won't go to the doctor."

Jimmy, who was backslidden at the time, dropped his head and left. When he got home, he told his wife that they needed to get back in church.

The next morning, Juanita and the children were back building fence. She was completely healed.

Jimmy and wife both got back in church and were there until death took them. Juanita said it was worth all the pain to see them saved and really living for God for over 20 years.

# Children

I have always loved babies and children. As a child, I daydreamed of having lots of twins and maybe triplets or quads. I had about 25 beautiful names picked out that I wanted to use. Of course, I wanted all girls. I even had names picked out for quads. I loved flower names: Rose, Lily, Iris, Pansy, Aster, Daisy, and others.

The thought hit me that they could all be boys. I didn't like boys. Boys were mean. All except one. I loved him. I could always trust Sterling. But what if I had triplet boys? I could name them for weeds: Smartweed, Ragweed, Crabgrass and Thistle. I could call them Smarty, Rags, Crabby and Pistol. It would probably fit them.

I was nearly 20 when I got married. Soon and very soon, I learned our happy life of a big family of 15 would not happen. He wanted zero kids.

Before our little boy was born, my husband sent me home. Where had my happy big family escaped? My husband married again and had another little boy less than two years after our marriage. All my dreams of little girls were gone.

One evening, I had a heavy, bitter time. How could I cope with maybe 50, 60 or maybe even 70 years alone? I could, at best, have Charles 20 years. Then what? I had pneumonia before he was born. Why couldn't I have died? It would have been over. There would have been no orphan baby to raise without a father to guide him. I would have rather had my casket than that awful word "divorced."

That night, I picked up my baby, laid him on the bed, got on my knees, put my head down on my baby, and called on God (my only help). Oh, I had Daddy, Mother, sisters, and brother at home. But they couldn't help my torn heart. I don't know how long it took. An hour or four? But I came through it the winner. I had a determined mind and wanted God's will. God blessed me that night.

I still wanted girls and a family. I tried to adopt. There were lots of babies to give away, but they wanted them placed in a two-parent home. One day, I came home discouraged again. I failed again in trying to get two little girls that were to be given away.

"Forget it," Daddy said, "I feel there are three little girls who are to be sent our way."

Not long after that, Bro. Simmons brought Brenda, his 10-year-old granddaughter, to church. Hazel fell in love with her and thought she could help her. Brenda had two sisters in Tupelo Children's Mansion, a home for orphans. They were coming to their grandparents as soon as school was out. Hazel started keeping Brenda every weekend. When the other two came home, they all came to our house for the summer.

Their little brother lived with his grandparents already. Then their mother came home to Mama to live. The girls wanted to live with us. One evening, after church, I was sitting in the car when Ruby, one of the girls, came to the car and gave me a hug and kiss before getting in the back seat.

"Ruby, there is your real mother sitting over there alone," I said. "Don't you think you should give her a hug and a kiss?"

She bounced up and said, "Okay, I'll go love her."

She came back crestfallen.

"What's the matter?" I asked.

"Mama said to don't be slobberin' on her," Ruby said. "Keep my slobbers to myself."

"Forget it," I said. "You can give me a hug and kiss any time you want."

"Can I call you mother?" Ruby asked.

"You sure can."

Many years have passed. Ruby's name was changed to Rita Kay at adoption. Hazel raised Brenda and I took the other two. Brenda called me "Mother," the same as Rita Kay and Linda, but she referred to Hazel as "Mama."

Brenda said she got the best. She had two mothers.

# Holy Ghost for Children

Bro. Simmons did not believe children could receive the Holy Ghost. I knew they could. I was nine, nearly 10, and Hazel was five. I was praying with Hazel when she got it, or when she realized she had it. There was no doubt.

Bro. Simmons said children belong to the Lord, so they already have it.

"Do they have to lose it then in order to receive it as the Bible says?" I asked.

He had no answer.

Our church was drifting. No one was coming to the Lord. Someone said the Lord laid on them a 30-day fast for the church. God moved after the fast was over. Bro. Simmons was up front on his knees praying. The pastor's six or seven children were on the front bench.

One of the four-year-old twins stood to her feet, raised her hands, and started speaking plainly in tongues. Right in Bro. Simmons' face. He sat on his knees and watched her.

"I don't care what anyone says, children *can* get the Holy Ghost," Bro. Simmons said. "If she didn't get it, then I don't have it."

That was the beginning of a Holy Ghost revival.

# Singing by Nate

Bro. Simmons and my daddy were both educated in note singing. They could take a book and sing the song written in the book by the shape of the notes. But they needed the tone of the first note to start them off.

Sis. Whitefield played the piano well but only by ear. She never knew in what key she played. Daddy and Bro. Simmons fussed over the key in which she played. Bro. Norris also knew the piano notes.

The fuss became hotter and hotter. As I sat in the congregation, I suddenly heard the devil laugh. It was scary, hideous. I had never heard anything like it. I started crying. We were supposed to be praising God in worship with singing. The devil was laughing at us. Pastor Whitfield asked me what was wrong.

"The devil is laughing at our confusion," I said. "I heard him. It's awful."

He walked back to the front and spoke.

"The devil is laughing at us," he said. "Sis. Ava just heard him. It's time to pray and praise God."

Everyone started asking forgiveness, praising God, and praying. Confusion turned into love, praising, and prayer. I never heard any more about "note singing" after that.

# Money From the Pop Machine

Linda, Rita Kay, and I were on our way to visit Juanita in Louisiana. We were tired and thirsty when we came upon a station that was open early.

We went to the pop machine for drinks. I put in a dollar. Drinks were 25 cents. When I pushed the button for a drink, the machine spit out around $3 in change. I got the girls' drinks, found the attendant, and asked who managed the pop machine. The attendant pointed to another guy.

"I put in a dollar and when I pushed the button for my drinks, this came out," I said to the other guy while showing him the money. "It isn't mine."

He reached out his hand. I dropped the money in it, turned, got in the car, and drove on. The girls watched him. He stood with his hand out and the money in it as far as they could see.

He was stunned at someone being honest.

# What Was Behind the Cemetery?

I was taking Delores' foster twins home after keeping them two weeks. We were nearly to El Dorado on Highway 167. Back then, it was a narrow blacktop,

I had one three-year-old in the back with Rita Kay, the other in the front with Linda. I got sleepy, pulled to the side of the road, and went to sleep behind the wheel. A car with two young men stopped and asked if I was having trouble. I explained that I just got a little sleepy.

"Well, I don't like you sitting along the road like that," one of them said. "There is a nice place where you can sort of camp half a mile back behind the cemetery."

I told them I would drive on. They stayed right behind me. The more they followed me, the more uneasy I felt. They started to pass me. Good! But when they got even with us, they tried to stop us. I wouldn't look their way. They stayed neck-to-neck with my truck, driving south in the northbound lane for about two miles.

I prayed and trusted God but was still scared. Finally, they stepped on the gas and went on. I watched every crossroad and driveway until daylight. I certainly wasn't sleepy anymore. Neither was Linda.

Why shouldn't I trust God with my life? He is better to me than I can tell. I love Him so!

# Wanda's Wedding

Wanda was getting married. Everyone wanted to be a part of it. She chose four bridesmaids and a matron of honor. Danny selected five groomsmen. Wanda's uncle, Ben, was set to perform the ceremony.

We only had six weeks to prepare. Linda got very sick and lost 20 pounds. She didn't have it to lose. I had to make her dress over again. I had to make Daddy a suit to give the bride away. Wanda had no daddy who cared to do it.

The wedding was to be in Lafayette, Indiana. I took the girls to Mildred's in Indianapolis early so I'd be close if needed. I had my girls and Daddy all fitted for the Saturday afternoon wedding. Early Friday morning, something suddenly woke me. "Juanita needs you," I left the girls with Mildred and took off for Lafayette. When I got there, Juanita was crying at the sewing machine.

"I've got the flower girl's basket to decorate, her headpiece to make, the candlelighters' headpieces to make…" Juanita said. The list went on.

"Whoa!" I said. "Give me the jobs one at a time. I can't remember that many."

Then I looked at her. She looked sick.

"Are you all right?" I asked.

"No, but I've got to do all this before I can lie down," Juanita said. The wedding is tomorrow."

I never thought God cared about clothes and fancy stuff. But I know he cares about His people. Juanita and Wanda were certainly two of His chosen. I knew for sure then that God had awakened and spoken to me to get up and go.

The bridesmaid dresses had old-fashioned hoop skirts. Mildred's husband was to bring the metal for the hoops from his work. All the dresses were done but the hoops.

All was ready when the music started upstairs for the wedding. I was downstairs pinning the hoops in my girls' dresses. There wasn't time to sew them in. But each girl was ready in time to walk. It was a beautiful wedding.

After the wedding, Juanita went to bed with the Hong Kong flu. She died in our home in Arkansas six weeks later. She was 47.

God had taken her as He promised her a little over 20 years before.

# Sleepy

One night, I was traveling with Linda and Rita Kay and got very sleepy. The two girls were supposed to take turns sitting in the front seat so they could keep me awake by talking. But it was Linda's turn, and she was also sleepy. What can you talk about when you are sleepy?

Finally, I was so sleepy that I got a crazy idea. Linda was always scared of everything. Even her own shadow. If I could scare her, she would stay awake.

There was a car behind me about a quarter mile back. I was doing the speed limit. I guess he was, too.

"Linda, what do you think about that car behind us?" I asked. "It has been following us for about 20 or 30 minutes. He just keeps the same distance."

Linda immediately awakened and stayed awake watching that car until daylight.

It worked.

There is no sleepier time than driving a car loaded with people who are all asleep.

# Hurry

Linda, Rita Kay, and I were traveling at night with our poodle dogs. I always preferred to travel at night. I usually never got sleepy. There was less traffic and less hassle.

We stopped at a well-lit rest area at 1 a.m. Nobody was there. Leisurely, we walked our dogs and then went to the restroom. Suddenly, I got in a hurry.

"Come on, girls," I said. "We've got to get out of here. Come on now!"

"But I need to wash my hands," Linda said.

"No!" I shouted. "Get in the car. Hurry!"

I pulled her from washing her hands. We ran to the car, got in, and locked all the doors. When I heard the doors lock, I took an easy breath and saw a truck coming up the ramp. The truck was a state truck. The driver and passenger talked for a minute then got out at the same time. Still, I waited. They walked up the walk together. Then, one man went in the men's room and the other in the door we just exited.

I turned to Linda and said, "Linda, what's the hurry?"

"I'm sorry, Mother," Linda said. "I'll never disobey you again."

# CHAPTER 6
## The 1970s

# Cancer

Mother seemed to be feeling poorly. She worked slower. She wouldn't sit at the table with us. She said she would rather get whatever any of us needed. But she wouldn't sit. She laid down a lot. Sometimes when she was cooking or washing dishes, she sat on the edge of a high stool. I was worried. She didn't seem to have any energy.

"Mother, what's wrong?" I asked.

"I'll be all right," she said.

I asked Daddy.

"Your mother has a problem," he said.

Yes, I knew that. Anyone with half a brain would know she had a problem. But what? I kept pushing them for an answer until Mother finally told me.

"I have a sore and I can't sit down," Mother said.

She finally let me see it. It was a blackish open sore about an inch across with dark red swelling about six inches across. I knew at first glance.

The family banded together and fasted and prayed. It got to the point where she could hardly walk anymore.

One night after they went to bed, I heard Daddy talking.

“I feel you are healed of your cancer,” Daddy told Mother.

The next morning. the scab came off. She didn’t go to the doctor, so we have no proof of what she had. But she had a family history of cancer. She lived to 93.

God has been very good to our family.

# Donnie Stine

Wanda gave birth to eight children: Deanna, Daniel, Donald, Darla, Donita, Dejuana, Dara, and David. She never had a doctor for any of them. They were all born at home with her husband and a midwife.

Little Deanna died of a tragedy at home when she was eight months.

One day, Donnie got sick at his stomach. He was throwing up and had a high fever. He couldn't or wouldn't eat. He got weaker and sicker. People started pushing Wanda to take him to the doctor, but she did not want to do that. She was raised on faith and had trusted God all her life.

All the busybodies kept warning Wanda that all her children could be taken from her if Donnie died. The busybodies should have been helping her pray. She eventually decided to take him to the doctor, but God stopped her.

"If you take him to the doctor, he will die." God spoke to Wanda.

So, she didn't take him. She sat beside him day and night praying, except when his daddy (Danny) could do it. I think it was nine days. She was so tired, but faithful to her son and to God.

A small lump of pus came up in the middle of his belly. Danny kept a close watch on it. The yellow lump began to look like a big pimple and grew larger. Danny wanted to pick it open. He asked Wanda what to do.

“Do what you want to do,” Wanda said. “Whatever you think best. I’m praying and I don’t want to see it.”

Danny went back to Donnie, took his fingernails, and pulled the top off the pimple. Pus shot over a foot high. Immediately, his high fever started to break. The odor was unbearable. He had been in a sort of a coma. Danny tried to clean him up, but Donnie was too weak to put in the bathtub. By morning, Donnie was completely back to himself, and the lump had quit draining.

Donnie had gone over a week without food and was hungry. Wanda wanted to give him soup or something light. Donnie wanted a Big Mac. And he got one. He ate every bit and was all right.

The couch on which he laid had to be burned. The odor was so bad, even with all their cleaning. It took weeks to get the odor from the house.

Only my God can do a miracle like that.

# Honor

My brothers, Jimmy and Robert, were talking very derogatory about our precious daddy one day. Yes, Daddy was older, forgetful, and very firm on Bible truths. The Lord always came first to the end.

Ben, Hazel, and I listened as the two of them brought up many things that supposedly happened before Daddy was saved and everything after that. Finally, Ben decided he'd heard enough.

"That may be all true," Ben said. "I don't know. But HE IS MY DADDY!"

Ben, the youngest living of six boys, had Exodus 20:12 in his mind and heart. "Honor they father and thy mother, that thy days may be long..."

"Robert, what do you think you'll be like at Daddy's age?" Hazel asked.

"Are you kidding?" Robert asked. "I'll be pushing up daisies."

And he was.

Jimmy lived to be 72. Robert lived to be 81. Ben is 90.

Honor your father and your mother. It pays off.

# Fun Time in Indiana

Danny and Wanda lived off Highway 52 south of Lafayette, Indiana. They bought property with a big creek running on the north edge and a steep hill on the south. The buildings were on level ground. The driveway to the four-lane highway was steep. It had snowed, melted and frozen again. The driveway made a perfect slide. The children, especially Donnie, played nonstop in the driveway.

Wanda was afraid they were getting too cold. She called them to come inside. Donnie begged to stay outside. Wanda started to let him play a little longer, but then hesitated and said no. She promised Donnie he could go back outside after eating and warming up a bit.

As they took their coats off, they heard a racket outside. A car started up the hill on 52, lost control, and made a complete spin around in the spot where the children were playing. They all were thankful as they watched the car pull away. And then they all went on playing.

# Runaway Donnie

Donnie was about five when he decided he wanted to go live with this great grandpa over 700 miles away.

"Mommy, I want to run away," Donnie said. "I want to live with Grandpa."

She talked and begged, but it didn't help.

"Okay," she said. "But I don't want you on that busy highway. I'll take you the two miles to the other road we take to Grandpa's."

He got in and they drove the two miles. When she turned on the lesser highway, she stopped. Donnie sat still.

"Well, Donnie, you need to kiss Mommy goodbye," she said. "It's a long way. It will probably take you two or three weeks to get there. Have Grandpa write and tell me when you get there."

Donnie came around the car, gave her a kiss goodbye, and then started walking fast down the edge of the road. The farther he walked, the slower his pace. Suddenly, he ran back to the car.

"Did you forget something?" she asked.

"Mommy, I don't want to go," Donnie said. "Can I go back home with you?"

That was the last of the running away.

# Daddy's Temper

"Let all bitterness, and wrath, and anger, and clamour, and evil speaking, be put away from you, with all malice. (Ephesians 4:31)

My daddy had a very bad temper. He always worked in or owned a garage of some kind. He was a young man working under a car. Someone came in and accused him of stealing. My daddy was not a thief, but he came near being a murderer. He had a big wrench in his hand and came out from under that car at top speed, intending to throw the wrench through the man.

"Wait!" the man screamed. "I'm probably mistaken."

Daddy cooled right down and was forever thankful he didn't kill him in a fit of anger. From that day on, Daddy fought to keep his temper under control. But he didn't yet have God to help him.

I was born with a temper just like his. There have been three times in my life that I didn't control it. One of those times happened when I was a paper hanger painter. They call it an interior decorator now.

People usually paid me by check instead of cash. Back in the 50s and 60s, a check was the same as money. I took a check I received and paid the electric bill. The clerk ran the check through to stamp it, gave me back the change and receipt, but failed to stamp my payment book. When I went to pay my bill the next month, I asked the lady to stamp the one from last month.

"I didn't stamp it because you didn't pay it," she said.

I showed her the receipt that she had given me.

"I didn't give you that receipt," she said. "You could have gotten that anywhere."

"I'll pay today for this month's bill, but not last month's," I said.

I was getting mad. My temper was near boiling. I left and called Opal Wise, the lady who wrote me the check the prior month. She told me she had gotten her checks from the bank and the one she wrote me was in it. It was stamped on the back by the electric company. She let me borrow it to take to the electric company.

I was so mad, never once thinking of putting away all anger. They tried to cheat me! I stomped in and slapped the check down on the counter.

"This is the check that I paid the electric bill with," I said. "And there is YOUR stamp on the back of it. Now stamp my receipt book!"

"Well, don't get so mad," the clerk said after stamping my payment book.

"No, I don't need to get so mad," I said in a not-so-quiet voice. "But you sure would have made me pay it again if I hadn't brought the check back."

I looked around and the room was full of people. I was ashamed.

I began to repent as I left the room. I certainly wasn't a witness for God with a temper like that. I hear people testify to what the Lord has brought them out of. I've heard them say, "Oh, I wish I could have been in church all my life like Sister Ava and not have to repent of so many things."

Praise God for being a forgiving God. I'm no better than the drunk that God has forgiven. I'm not perfect, but still trying to be.

My Bro. Ben would say, "I know you are trying. Very trying."

# John Whitfield

Hazel's five-year-old son had just been adopted and became one of us. I leaned over to hug him, and he jumped up and threw his arms around my neck and his legs around my lower hip. I heard and felt my back snap. After about two weeks of hobbling around, I was back in church.

John Whitfield was about 16. He was in the spirit and came and just touched my back. I was immediately healed.

That was the beginning of his ministry. He got a job at Harp's Supermarket in Mountain Home, Arkansas. He worked with a lot of worldly boys who told dirty jokes and used filthy language. John was a hard worker but talked about Jesus to everyone. Many people came to the store just to get John to pray for them. When he prayed, they were healed, either in the store or in the parking lot. One day, the boss took John aside.

"John, many are complaining about your talking about God all the time," his boss said.

John reached behind him and untied his apron. The boss kept talking.

"John, can't you just let up a little?" he asked. "Many of the boys are complaining."

"I have to listen to their filthy jokes while I eat every day or have a break," John said. "If I can't talk about my Jesus and how good He is to me, then you can have your job. God will give me another."

John handed the boss his apron.

"John, you are my best worker," the boss said. "Please stay and talk about your God all you want."

The boss handed back the apron. John's ministry grew from that point. He married Anne, a sweet Holy Ghost girl who helped him instead of pulling him down. They had three children.

John and Anne took a sister home from church. Their children were not with them. As they were going back home, a drunk hit them head on, killing both. Harp's Supermarket closed and locked the doors the afternoon of the funeral. Most of Mountain Home closed their business during the funeral.

I think the drunk got five years. He is out and still drinking.

# The Painter

Hazel was a painter for Baxter General Hospital for years. She loved it and they all loved her.

She started with empty patient rooms. She filled all the holes, sandpapered where needed, and then painted. Hazel told her boss, Bill Short, that she loved painting, but really did not like patching the holes. She naturally would do it because it was part of her job.

One day, Hazel stepped into the office for something. She heard Mr. Short talking.

"Hazel has a lot of patching in that room," Mr. Short said to another man in the room. "She told me that one of the things she really loved to do is patch holes."

"That is a factitious fabrication!" Hazel said.

Hazel loved playing with big words. Nothing like me on that.

"Did she say that I lied?" Mr. Short asked.

"I think that's what she said!" the other man said.

They had her paint stripes in the parking lot and joked about having her paint the flagpole. She told them they didn't have a long enough ladder.

She finished a job one day and came in for orders. Mr. Short was out. The next person in charge told her to paint the air conditioner on top of the hospital. He told her where to turn it off, then paint it all but the motor. She turned it off, got on the flat roof, crawled into the air conditioner, and started painting. It was about a half-day job.

Mr. Short came back, not knowing the orders that Hazel had been given. He saw the air conditioner switched off. The air conditioner was supposed to be on all the time. He reached to turn it on but stopped short of doing it.

Policy dictated that the switch be sealed and red taped if anything was wrong. It wasn't, but Mr. Short felt the need to investigate further. He went outside and saw a ladder up against the building. And up on top there sat his little painter inside the air conditioner, happily painting away! He exploded.

"Don't you know when you turn off a big switch like that you are supposed to red tag it?" Mr. Short asked.

"What's red tag?" Hazel responded. "I've never heard of red tagging anything."

He nearly fainted.

"I almost killed you," Mr. Short said. "I started to turn on the switch, but I didn't. If I had, you wouldn't be here."

The man who told her to turn off the switch was supposed to do it himself and red tag it.

God used Mr. Short to take care of His own. God is so good to us.

# Daddy Left Us

When mother was in the hospital with her first broken hip, Daddy talked to Dr. Snow, the head doctor and county coroner. He let the nurses take his vital signs and they wanted to put him in the hospital. His blood pressure was too high, and his heart wasn't beating right. He was 87.

"I know I haven't long to live," Daddy told the doctor. "I don't want anything done for me. I don't want my wife and family held responsible for anything. I know and they know what I want. Can you help me get what I want?"

Dr. Snow agreed.

Daddy had been working in the shop, making pig troughs for a neighbor farmer. He came in for breakfast and picked up the Bible to read while waiting. He then dropped the Bible.

"Mama, will you pick up my Bible?" he asked. "I can't seem to pick it up."

Mother went over to him and saw his arm dangling. She picked up the Bible and gave it to him in his right hand.

"You've had a stroke," she told Daddy.

"They tell me when a person has a stroke to work it off," Daddy said. "Get the limbs working again. I'm going to my bedroom to get a piece of that candy Ava bought for me."

He got out of his chair and started. Mother noticed his left leg was dragging. She took him by the dangling arm and went with him. Mother hadn't been out of the hospital with her broken hip but about eight weeks. When they got to the bedroom, he had another stroke. Mother gave him a shove over on the bed with him trying to help. They got him in bed. He weighed 220 pounds.

I was not home at the time. Hazel, Jason, and I had gone to work on Hazel's basement. Mother called Hazel's neighbors to get us home. When we got home, Hazel called Dr. Snow.

"Let him die at home," Dr. Snow said. "That is what he wants. Give him the best care possible. Call if you need me."

Daddy never ate the breakfast or the piece of coconut candy. When I gave him cold water, he choked as he always did on the first swallow.

"Just like usual," he said. "Open my mouth and pour it down my windpipe."

He once got his feet tangled in the blanket. He asked Mother if she could pick up some of the junk from the floor, because he couldn't "work in all the mess." Mother straightened his blanket, and he was fine.

I sat by his bedside wishing I could do something. I loved him so. He picked up my hand.

"Whose hand have I got?" he asked.

I told him it was mine.

Then with his right hand, he found his left hand.

"Now whose hand do I have?" he asked.

"Daddy, you've had a stroke," I said. "That is your hand. It is no good right now."

He picked it up with his right hand and threw it as far as a fastened hand could be thrown.

"If it's no good, throw it away!" he said.

We tried to get him to drink some Ensure, but he spit it out and said he didn't want that "slop!"

In about four or five days, Arlo, the family troublemaker, called Dr. Snow.

"My dad is down with a stroke in his home," Arlo told him. "They are just letting him die with no care. Is there anything I can do about it?"

Dr. Snow told him there was nothing anyone could do but carry out his wishes.

"He knew he was about to go," Dr. Snow said. "I assure you, he is getting the best care 24 hours a day."

We never knew how Arlo found out.

On Aug. 5, 1979, Daddy suffered a fatal third stroke just one week after the first.

Oh, how I loved my daddy. I still miss him.

# God Has the Answer

Danny and Wanda had six children when tragedy struck. It was a snowy Sunday afternoon in Indiana. It was good for sledding. Their family loved it.

Danny, the perfect father (if ever there was one), took all the kids out to play. Deanna, 8 months, was in a backpack on his back. She fell asleep after a while, so Danny took her inside. Wanda took her from the backpack and laid her on the bed. She went on sleeping. The top blanket binding was off about 18 inches.

It came time to get ready for evening service. Wanda stepped in the next room to get the baby who had, in her sleep, scooted under the blanket binding, turned, and slid off the bed. Wanda said Deanna was on her knees with her head against the side of the bed, and the binding around her neck. It was too late. She was gone. Just a few minutes too late. Wanda was devastated.

Then the law stepped in. Social services believed it was foul play.

Wanda's older brother, David, married a millionaire and was well thought of in the community. David decided he'd had enough with that foul play narrative. He went to the social services office mad.

"Lay off my sister," David demanded. "She loved that baby as we all did. She took the best care of her children. I don't want to hear anymore, or I'll have you sued."

Social services laid off.

Wanda couldn't be comforted. Nothing anyone could say or do helped…until God gave her a vision. She saw her deceased mother with Deanna in her arms.

"Thank you, Jesus," Wanda said. "Mamma can care for her better than I could."

After that, she never seemed to grieve.

# Taskmasters

As Daddy grew nearer to the end of life, he grew more concerned about the ones of his household.

"Where did you go?" "Why were you late?" "Are you alright?" "If you have trouble, call home."

I was 40 years old and lived in my own travel trailer. Hazel was 34. She adopted Jason and was preparing her own home. We understood that Daddy was concerned for our welfare. We tried our best to keep him happy, as we knew his time was getting short.

Hazel's worktime varied according to what she happened to be doing. If painting inside the hospital, she tried mostly to work at night. But all outside painting had to be done in daylight. I worked nights and got off at 7:30 a.m. and was supposed to be home by 8:15. If I wasn't, Daddy thought something was wrong. I had to tell him if I planned to make any stops on the way home or he would worry. That was fine. He was 87. We understood. But when he passed on, things didn't change.

My foster brother, who was my pastor, decided he needed to run our business. We couldn't buy anything or do anything without his approval. He was so difficult. For a while, I stayed with friends, and he didn't know my whereabouts/

Then I got very sick. Too much pressure on my nerves. I vomited at work. They took me to the hospital. I had ulcers because of my nerves.

“Of all people, I never would have thought you had a nerve problem,” Dr. Snow said. “You always seemed so calm.”

He didn’t know what I was going through.

Meanwhile. Pastor wanted to get more converts in the church. He decided to hold a brush arbor meeting. They built the brush arbor where we planned to build our church. I was usually the first one at church, so likewise the brush arbor meeting. I sat in the end chair about halfway back and silently prayed. I felt like a stranger.

I thought someone came up behind me and put their hand on my shoulder. I turned to see what they wanted. No one was there, but I felt the comforting hand. From that day on, I claimed “He Touched Me” as my song. There was comfort, but no let up on the pressure. In about three months, He spoke to me. “Go.” I knew I heard a voice clear enough but didn’t realize it was God. I turned back to what I was doing. He spoke again, but this time louder “Go.”

“Yes, Lord,” I said.

That was late at night after church. By the next morning, I was on my way, not knowing where. I had my old van. No heater.

Leave? My new house a little over half done? My furniture? My good job? My sister?

God said go. So, at 51 years of age, I left. I packed in my van a few clothes, all my bedding and blankets, and a few pans and dishes. I took my little rocking chair, accordion, and my poodle Kooki. I stopped for a day or two to see my only cousin I knew in Illinois. Then I planned to drive to Mildred's and see mother in Indianapolis before heading south.

I was weak and sick. I didn't figure I had long to live. I had a daughter in Palatka, Florida. I planned to head her direction. She had no idea I was on my way.

"Jesus, you guide my way," I said. "I'm just a sick old woman. Guide me where You want me to stop. Make my old van go as far as you want. Let it need repair before going on. I'll know that is where you want me. For now."

Mildred tried to detain me for a while, but I was determined to press onward.

Church was just letting out when I arrived in Palatka on Sunday morning. No one knew me except Arvel and Rita Kay. We visited a while in the church yard. It was a beautiful day. I asked my son-in-law Arvel to look at my van. Something went wrong with the steering at the edge of Palatka.

"Now, I want everyone to hear this," Arvel told the people in the church yard. "There is no way I will ever disagree with my mother-in-law. If she can drive that van, she could knock me flat."

He was over six feet and over 300 pounds. I was 5'1" and 120.

Arvel said the tie rods were just about to fall off. It was the end of the first lap of my journey. After about two years, I moved with Hazel and Jason to Hollister, eight miles west.

I can see now that God was leading me to where I am today.

As a result of the move, I landed in a new church that I've attended for over 30 years while sitting under Pastor Raney, Pastor Gowan, Pastor Nelms, and now Pastor Little.

# CHAPTER 7
## The 1980s

# Games

Playing games is fun and harmless. It's just something to do while getting together for fellowship if everyone plays fair. I have a niece who practices witchcraft and tried to use her power on both Hazel and me, but our God was bigger than that. One UPC minister in Terre Haute, Indiana tried to cast the devil out of her. But she stood up to him and said, "May the best devil win." She turned and walked away. The minister died that night. No one knew why. He "just died."

Hazel was keeping my niece's two oldest children, Bobbie and Carol, and sending them to Christian school. One evening the children were playing Uno. Hazel's adopted son and Bobby were losing every game. After winning several games, Carol spoke.

"My mama is a witch," she said. "And I can do it too. I can see through the cards and know what you have."

Hazel got rid of the cards. I think she should have gotten rid of the girl instead. Hazel never played Uno again. I don't enjoy games as much as I love getting together for fellowship.

I don't believe in cheating. Train up a child in the way he should go. According to the dictionary, cheating is a form of lying. How can you teach your children to be honest if we are not honest in our fun? Hazel loved playing games, but she would not play a game if she knew a cheating person was playing.

When I was younger, I would get mad inside if I didn't win. I tried not to show it, but I did. I just quit playing games for years. I needed to crucify the flesh and get control of myself. When I got myself under control where it made no difference if I won or lost, I started playing again. The other night, I played with the pastor, his wife and Barbara. Pastor won the first three games. I got joy out of seeing his happiness.

"I hope he wins them all," I said to Barbara. "It makes him so happy."

He ultimately won four and Barbara two.

If I can't be happy about a game, then I'll chuck the game (and be happy).

# That Daddy of Mine

'Twas a long time ago, but I just can't forget
The Daddy I had. I love him, you bet!
But some things about him, that was hard at the time
Now I wish I'd done more for that Daddy of mine.

I wanted to clean, but "Do not move those"
That's the shoes that he wears whenever he goes
Out to the shop to putter or work
He had to do and never did shirk.

He'd work hard all day, although he was old
But things had to be done. That's what we were told
I'm too tired to bathe, so I'll just go to bed
What matters the pillow, where I lay down my head
It's my pillow you see, So why should you care?
It doesn't matter to me if there's grease in my hair

"Sure my room is dirty, but it's mine just the same
I didn't start out for fortune or fame
Now don't move those papers. I have them all right."
Although to us, 'twas a terrible night.

I'll eat all my meals in my nice easy chair
What matters the crumbs, the dog is right there.
She'll pick up the crumbs, though the spots there will stay
He couldn't see them and didn't care anyway.

But now he is gone! I can clean every bit
Do as I please and he won't throw a fit
I can go when I want and come back any day
And I haven't a dad to say "yea" or "nay."

I was good to my daddy while he was here
I'm sure glad I was. Makes him seem very near.
I miss him so much that I wish I could see
Some spots on the floor not put there by me.

Some shoes in my way or some grease on the bed
A pillow that's dirty where he lay down his head
But those days are over. I'll see them no more
No junk in my way. No tools on the floor.

Now if you have a loved one who makes you to fret
Be nice to them here and you'll never regret.
Don't worry about spots or things that not fine
Remember I told you of that daddy of mine.

# Pay to Help Me

I was driving on Highway I-10, coming home from visiting Charles. I had a flat tire. I got out to change it, and a young man stopped behind me. He looked like a happy chap or just a boy who didn't care much about details.

"Got a spare?" he asked. "I'll change it."

I just stood and watched. After he changed it, he reached in his pocket and took out a $20 bill.

"Here," he said. "I feel you need this."

I was dumbfounded! I tried to thank him. He gave a wave, got in his car and was gone. That's the only time I ever got paid to let someone else change a tire.

I believe God loves me. He knew I needed it.

# Hazel's Bad Fall

Because of problems, I quit my good job, left my new house, and went to Florida. Arkansas never seemed like home to me anymore. I believe God told me twice to go, but just like most children, I had to be told more than once.

Hazel said she would follow to Florida me in a year. I had been gone almost a year when Jason's school closed. Her new pastor didn't believe in Christian schools.

"Children who go to public school have to learn early to fight off sin and live for God," the pastor said.

I've seen parents who dedicate their babies to God. Years later, they jerk them from God and send them to public school for the devil to raise.

One day, Hazel took Sis. Nita to Little Rock for a doctor's appointment. Without notice, the pastor walked into the Christian school and made demands while Hazel was away from home.

"Close the school now!" the pastor said. "Send or take all the children to their homes. Tell them to put them all in public school!"

Hazel returned home to find a school worker had taken her six-year-old son and his two cousins, six and eight, to her house with no one home. The children walked a short distance to the Whitfields where Sis. Nita had left her 12-year-old daughter with her two younger sisters. That left the 12-year-old child taking care of five children instead of two small ones.

Hazel sent the two cousins home to Indiana, put in a two-weeks' notice at work, put her son Jason in a Baptist school for two weeks and prepared to move to Florida. When she got to Florida, she stored her furniture in my son-in-law's garage and moved in with me into a singlewide, two-bedroom mobile home.

Hazel didn't get work quickly, so Arvel gave her and Jason the job of raking leaves and cleaning out the gutters. Hazel set her ladder on thick leaves. When she got up to the gutter to clean it, the ladder slid at the bottom. The left side hit the door casing and the right side hit the porch screen, throwing her to the rocks below. She broke her right shoulder and her left knee.

The shoulder had to be put in a sling and the knee got a bolt and a cast. It wasn't to be touched to the floor for three months. Hazel couldn't raise her arm to comb her hair or put her hand behind her back. Physical therapists applied lots of pressure on it three times a week. Nothing moved it, so they gave up and released her.

A few weeks later, our church went to a fellowship service out of town. Of course, I couldn't go. My job caused me to always stay home. Hazel and Jason went with the McColskeys. At the service, the minister said for everyone to raise their hands. Of course, Hazel tried.

"If this ain't a fine way to raise my hands to praise the Lord." Hazel said.

The right hand suddenly shot up equal to the other. When she got home, she was still raising her hands and praising the Lord. Then she went back to the doctor when it was time to check the bolt in her knee. While there, she witnessed about her shoulder.

“My arm is all right,” she said. “God healed it.”

The doctor doubted her.

“It’s right here in the book,” the doctor said. “The arm is set and will never move.”

“But I told you God healed it,” Hazel said. “It’s all right.”

She put her hand on her head and then behind her back.

“But it can’t be all right,” the doctor said, referring again to what was written in the medical book.

Finally, he shook his head and acknowledged that she had shown proof of healing.

“God can do anything,” Hazel said.

I wonder what the doctor wrote in his book.

# One Rose

Isn't it something what a rose can do?
It can give you a lift when you're down and blue.
I went to my van. I thought no one knew
How discouraged I was all through and through.

I'll tell you right now how the story goes.
There in my van seat I found a red rose.
It gave me life   to know someone cared
And left me a rose. It must be shared.

I picked up the rose, held it tenderly.
Could it do for others what it did for me?
I put it behind me and started away.
It was a beautiful rose on a beautiful day.

My friend was there in the old lawn chair.
So, I tucked the red rose in her pretty white hair
She looked really lovely, at least to me.
So I went on my way, feeling better you see.

So, then this morning as I did my task.
What became of the rose? I didn't ask.
There was the rose all pretty and red
Where her mother could see it as she lie in bed.

Our poor little Mommie can't get out and go.
How she stands it to lie there, I'll never know.
With nothing to cheer her day after day,
I'm glad my red rose was given her way.

# Blind

I was living in Palatka, Florida where I attended church with a blind lady and her two little boys. We were really having good church services. The lady claimed the Holy Ghost.

We prayed for her, and the spirit was so strong. I thought she would be healed. My faith was in it.

She sat in the front seat as I took her home after church. Apparently, she didn't get the healing. I was so disappointed. Suddenly, she gave a little cry and slid closer to me.

"What's wrong?" I asked her.

Everything seemed fine to me.

"That car was too close," she said.

"How do you know?" I asked. "Can you see?"

"Yes, and I don't want to," she said. "If I can see, then I'll lose my government check. Then what would we live on?"

She never saw again that I know of. I always believed she would go on as if she couldn't see, so she could keep her check. But God let it be known.

# TV in My Home

I had a job working for Sis. McColskey, the pastor's wife, in about 1983. Her mother was in failing health and had a TV she watched all the time.

I came in one day and told Sis. McColksey that I was quitting and moving.

"I'll take your mother with me if she wants to go," I said. "You can pay me what you are paying me now, you can care for her yourself, or you can put her in a nursing home."

Sis. McColskey said her mother preferred to go with me rather than a nursing home. When they started to move her, Sis McColskey said, "I'll sure be glad to get that TV out of my house."

"Well, it sure isn't coming in mine," I said.

"Oh, Mommy will have to have her TV," Sis. McColskey said. "What would she do all day without it.?"

"Well, there is no TV coming in my home," I said. "Just put her in a nursing home."

I went on moving my things. When I got back from moving a load, they had all decided she would be better off, and happiest with me, so she would do without TV. We kept her in our home until her death.

When I saw her health rapidly declining, I called Sis. McColskey. She just said to do the best we could. She didn't feel she had the strength to go through watching her mother pass away.

I called her brother who lived 30 miles away. He came but did not get there in time. A neighbor came and stayed with us so we wouldn't be alone.

The McColskeys and I stayed friends until her death. I sang at her funeral. They were my best friends for about eight years until we moved apart, and Sis. McColskey passed on.

# My Brother Jimmy

Jimmy was a tractor mechanic. He worked in a tractor garage for years but always had his own shop at home. He was 72. Perfect health. Pretty good eyesight. All his own good teeth. He had well set hair. He was very good looking. He was in church and doing well.

One day, Jimmy was at home in his shop using a blow torch. He shut it off and laid it on a drum nearby. Some say the drum was empty. Some say it was not. I wasn't there, so I don't know.

The drum exploded, burning all Jimmy's clothes off, except his belt and shoes. His daughter-in-law came running across the field after hearing the explosion and seeing the fire. He was naked and badly burned all over his body. He ran to the house, dropped to his knees at his living room recliner, and started speaking in tongues.

Jimmy spent two weeks in the burn center in Shreveport, Louisiana.

He lived 20 years for God after Juanita broke her foot, an incident that brought him and his wife back to God.

# Fire

Ben's daughter, Rita, and the family were canning on a cookstove in the yard. Joy, Rita's youngest daughter, was a teen. She had on a cotton skirt and polyester slip and blouse. The polyester clothes exploded because of intense heat coming from the canning stove. Her brother put out the fire with the garden hose. Her body was badly burned.

When the hospital dismissed her, the doctor said, "Joy, I'm so sorry about the bad scars on your body. I tried and did the best I could."

"Don't worry about that, doctor," Joy said. "I wear clothes."

What a great answer from a Christian girl.

# My Chickens

I needed a job, and a neighbor close by
Had an egg farm, and I wanted to try
To gather the eggs and run 'em and pack 'em.
Then, in the cooler, with hens I did stack 'em.

I asked for the job, but they weren't quite sure
A woman my age could really endure.
The work is quite hard, and the hours are long.
They weren't so sure that I was that strong.

They decided to try, so they put me inside.
I couldn't get out, even though I tried.
I wanted outside on the farm in the air.
It was dirty and dusty, but I didn't care.

So, then I went out, the eggs to gather
And never considered the changes of weather.
Sometimes it's raining, I get wet to the skin.
Then the sunshine is out, and I dry off again.

But still, it is fun, and the chickens a pleasure
And the joy in my work is much beyond measure.
The difference in chicks, are as people to me.
If you would just watch, you would soon see.

There is the old grouch, who pecks 'til it hurts
And the playful children, who pull at my skirts.
They untie my shoes, and ride on my back.
And then comes the rooster and gives me a "whack."

Some are afraid and they hurry away.
And others come to me all ready to play.
They all do some singing. But it's different, you know.
The white chicks sing high, while reds sing down low.

I think while they're singing, they're praising the Lord.
Everything that has breath, so saith the Word.
The trees clap their hands, the wind whispers a tune.
I wonder if they know He's coming real soon.

The animals rejoice and the mountains give praise.
But man in God's image forgets Him for days.
Let's take heed to the hen as onward we trod,
And lift happy voices in praise to our God.

# Snake at the Chicken House

My new job at the chicken farm required me to get there just before daylight. I was to close the curtains on the pullet houses so it would be dark inside, then open them at noon and go home. That meant sitting from daylight until noon with nothing to do. Nothing! I couldn't sit that long every day and do nothing.

The chicken farm was a mess. Lunch sacks, pop bottles, cans, plastic, boards, bricks, rocks. You name it. It was thrown around somewhere. I asked the owners if I could clean it up a bit. They said I could do what I wanted.

The next day, I cleaned up the place. I never left a thing. It all looked so nice. The next morning, I took my flashlight to close the first curtain. Right where I needed to stand was a big snake about 2.5 feet long and big around. It looked mean to me. There was not a rock, board, or stick around. Nothing. I cleaned up everything the day before. I stood still with the light shining on the snake.

"Lord, what can I do?" I asked. "Help me, Jesus."

The snake started to slither up the 4x4 on the corner of the chicken house. I jerked off my shoe and hit him on the head (I had a pair of slip-on wedgies with heavy wood heels). Then another rap and another and another until I was mighty sure he was dead. Jesus answered me when I asked for help.

I had tools in the van. I went and got my hammer and dragged the snake to the concrete around the pump (Genesis 3:15) on the concrete.

One of the bosses came about 10 o'clock.

"Who killed that snake?" he asked.

"I did it with my shoe," I said.

"Woman, don't you know that's a highland moccasin?" he asked.

"No, I didn't know," I said. "It was a snake and that's all I needed to know.

"That snake can kill you," he said.

"No, it can't," I said. "It's dead."

I told him about five times that morning the snake couldn't kill me because it's dead. It was the last of my job there. They sent me to a closer farm to be manager and they could keep an eye on me.

The next day, I met a man I didn't know in the grocery store. I'd rather meet a highland moccasin any day. At least I could kill and get rid of that snake. But a snake walking on two legs is a different matter.

But Jesus took care of both because I trusted in Him.

# Almost Robbed

Bro. McColskey wanted to start meetings in Madison, Florida. Someone gave him a piano. Someone else said he would move it for $50. I volunteered to pay the $50 when I got paid. I just started working on the chicken farm and my check was very small.

I picked up a few groceries. As I was signing my check, a man behind me said, "I know you."

I know he didn't know me.

"You're Ah—va," he said. "I need to talk to you," he said. "I'll meet you in the parking lot."

I backed up and stood waiting. He checked out, then went outside. I asked the cashier if she heard what the man said to me. She did not, but thought we were friends. I had never seen him before and had just moved to the area.

I went to the office and asked for a security officer to escort me outside. As we walked outside, I saw the man walk across the parking lot to my van. I think I was about to be robbed and I only had about $100.

I think I'd rather meet a highland moccasin.

# Busted Bubble

I was very happy, doing what I loved to do. My old van had been a repair van for a telephone company. There were no side windows, except the front doors. The back doors had small glasses and only two seats in the front. New carpet covered the floor.

I picked up five to eight children for church. They weren't always the same kids. All those, plus the ones who came with their parents, created a Sunday School class of usually 10 to 15 children.

I had three Spanish children, one girl and two boys who had no Christian upbringing. They spoke very good English, but their mother was still having problems. On the outside back of my van, I had a sticker with the words, "Jesus, My Joy of Living."

When taking the children home, I dropped off the Spanish children first. As soon as I pulled away from their house, the others told me that one of the Spanish boys made dirty finger signs to the cars following on the road behind us. Wow! The devil sure knew how to bust my bubble that time. I told the pastor and the child's mother.

What more could I do? What a witness with my sign of joy on the back.

# Accused of Cheating

My first chicken farm job required me to gather eggs twice a day. After the first morning gathering, I was supposed to run them in the washer/grader/weighing machine. I received five cents a dozen. I don't remember what I got for the other labor.

I had to count the eggs I gathered every time and write it down on the board. The night eggs were to be stacked on a table to be run the next morning with the morning eggs.

One morning, my boss, Joe Crain, met me when I got to work.

"You are writing down more eggs than you gather," he said.

"Let's go count them again," I said.

The eggs were in flats, every house kept separate. I think there were 10 houses. I stood there as he counted them. There were nine dozen with five eggs left over. He didn't count the five eggs. I did. I stopped him and told him to count those five. After counting the eggs in all the houses, it turns out I still had uncounted eggs left over for which I didn't get paid.

"Now, Joe, I try to live the life I talk about." I said. "If you can't trust me to be honest, then I quit. I wouldn't sell my soul for five cents."

His wife spoke up.

"You wouldn't go to hell for writing down too many eggs," Joe's wife said.

"Maybe you think you wouldn't, but I know I would," I said. "I know what is right."

# Thank You, Jesus

Hazel and I had a job together at the chicken farm. When full, we had 16 houses with 1600 chicks in each house.

We had to run to the main store for something two miles away. Hazel would do that while I fixed a quick lunch. It was a time when we were rushed. I grabbed the iron skillet from the oven and put it on the burner. The skillet and I stuck fast. I shook from head to toe. I knew it was the end. My life flashed before me. I kept a repented heart. I felt ready.

I still tried to pull loose but couldn't. Suddenly, I was free. I sat down because I was so weak. I couldn't raise my hand. I continued to thank God. Hazel came back, stood, and looked at me. I managed to get the words out: "Don't touch the stove." She still stood looking at me.

As I got stronger, I told her to turn off the breaker to the stove. She stepped to the breaker box.

"It's already off," she said.

Jesus turned it off to save my life.

# Isn't God Good?

Mildred was finishing her house, putting hardwood floors all over the upstairs except the bathroom. Someone figured the square footage and picked up the hardwood. She always wanted things ready.

She hired someone to put part of it down, but Mildred finally started doing it herself. She feared she would run out of flooring. The closer she came to finishing, the more she knew she wouldn't have enough. She didn't want to drive all the way back to pick up another bundle and then have that bundle almost all left over.

Without buying more, she had one board left over 11.5 inches long. She took her art wood burner and wrote on it, "Isn't God good?"

I have the plaque in my living room.

Just a daily reminder.

# CHAPTER 8

## The 1990s

# Fifty Dollars

Pastor Raney was still pastoring when we paid off the mortgage on the church. The carpet needed replacing badly. Pastor said we should donate what we could until we had enough to pay cash for it.

Bro. Ron Adkins ran a carpet store. He said he would put it down for his donation and let the church have the carpet at cost. Hazel and I had a truck payment, and we were driving from the chicken farm to church (40 miles one way) at least two or three times a week, so we had no extra money.

Hazel and I were talking about it as I was driving on Park Avenue in Valdosta after church one day.

"I wish we could help," I told Hazel. "But I can see no way now."

Then, suddenly, we saw a bill lying in the street. I stopped and she jumped out and got it. It was $50.

We went right back to the church and paid it on the carpet.

# Empty Gas Tank

I had a good little Dodge Ram 50 pickup truck. It made good gas mileage at over 30 miles to the gallon on a trip.

I was not always careful to watch my gas gauge. We were in South Arkansas, headed to see Sis. Moore, and then visit family. In the late evening, I looked at my gauge and it showed empty! We were on strange back roads. On and on we drove. Pitch dark. Still no station. I prayed. I'm sure Hazel did too.

Back then, it wasn't really dangerous to sit in our locked car all night. But what then? There were no stations. Just winding roads through the pine woods. I never went that way before or after.

Late in the night, we came to an open station. We put 12 and seven-tenths gallons in a 12-gallon tank.

I don't know how long God kept us running on fumes. I know the gas was all gone miles before.

God especially helps stupid, forgetful people like me.

Thank you, Jesus!

# A Broken Arm

Hazel and I were building a fence around our property. As I stepped down the hill, I caught my heel in a wisteria vine and fell backward down the hill in the front road ditch.

"Hurry and get up," Hazel shouted. "You're in a fire ant bed."

"I can't," I said. "I've broken my arm."

"Good!" she responded.

I didn't understand. Why would she think a broken arm was good? She thought I was going to say that I broke my hip. She was thankful it was my arm instead. And I was also thankful that I had killed the ant bed the day before. Hazel helped me up, but the pain was so bad I felt faint.

The pastor I had at that time didn't believe in going to the doctor for anything. Hazel called him. With cloth and strips of cardboard, he set it, but not right. For a week, I endured it, but I felt I could stand the pain no longer. I had my pastor unwrap it and try again. It was better, but still not right.

I went two more weeks wearing that wrap. When the pain was gone, the pastor removed the wrap. The arm was crooked. I didn't use it for a while because I didn't want to strain it and break it again.

When I told Mildred that the bandage came off in three weeks and I no longer had pain, she wanted to see my arm.

"Well, if it wasn't crooked, I'd say you didn't break it," Mildred said. "Because it couldn't be well that quickly."

Then I knew why God let it be crooked without pain. Just to prove His power.

People said I would develop severe arthritis in that arm, but I've had very little. Most of it is in my legs, back and right arm.

More proof of His power

Why would Mildred doubt? She was healed of her appendix instantly.

What He can do for you, He can do for me.

# Poor Fly

Hazel was keeping her foster granddaughter, Sherry, who had been passed from one parent to the other, from aunt, to grandparents, and then back to mamma or daddy. She really didn't know what house to call "home."

We were going somewhere, and a fly was in the car. Hazel rolled the window down and made the fly go out of the car.

"That's one fly that will never see home again," Hazel said.

About 10 minutes later, I noticed Sherry crying in the back seat. She wasn't making any noise, but tears streamed down her face.

"I was thinking of that poor fly that can never find home again," Sherry said.

We might think that's funny, but to a little girl who was continually torn from one home to the other, it was a serious matter.

Stop. Think of your little ones. Are you furnishing them with a secure, happy home or are they like the fly? They don't know where home is.

# CHAPTER 9

## 2000 to Present

# A Boy or a Man?

My foster nephew – Joel Whitfield's little boy – was playing with a little girl. They were both about four. They were trying to stand on a small log. If Alex got on, she would push him off and try to stand on it herself. She fell every time she tried, so Alex would get back on it. And the girl would push him off again. This went on for a long time. Finally, she hit him. He had enough and hit back.

His daddy had been watching, When Alex hit the little girl, he picked him up and spanked him. Others who saw it came to Alex's defense.

"That's not fair," they said. "She hit him first. He shouldn't have been spanked. She's the one who isn't playing fair."

"That is enough!" Joel said in a firm, but quiet voice. "I'm not raising her, and I'm not raising a little boy. I'm raising a man. If I allow my son to hit little girls, then I can expect my son to hit his wife. Now, I don't want to hear any more about it."

Alex is grown now and is about 20. He is very respectable to all, especially his mother and his older sister. Everyone speaks well of Joel's three children, Beth, Alex, and Ezra.

We need more fathers like Joel.

# Headache

Pastor Nelms had just become our pastor. One morning, I awoke with a bad headache. It started about where my backbone joined my head. It was bad, but as the days went on, it got worse. It hurt so bad I wrapped a feather pillow around my head and clamped my arms around it. I couldn't even get to the bathroom without help.

Hazel took me to church in my wheelchair. I could no longer walk. I had my cell phone and called Dr. Susan Harding to see if I could get a hospital bed so Hazel could care for me more easily. She sent a woman to see if I really needed one. The woman went back with a definite "yes," and reported that I needed to be examined.

Doctors wanted to put me in the hospital. I finally agreed to go for an examination. They admitted me and started running tests. Everything came out negative, but I was still getting worse. I could no longer sit up, much less walk. But lots of people were praying for me.

After a week in the Quitman hospital, I began to improve. I was on IVs, and they gave me two units of blood. But they still couldn't find what was wrong. They let me sit up in bed for five minutes, then let me stand and sit right back down. Then I could stand twice in one day. The headache was still there, but much better due to some strong medication.

My niece, who works in a hospital in Dallas, Texas, kept tabs on me. I don't know how. She called her dad in Arkansas.

"Daddy, please pray for Aunt Ava," my niece told her dad. "She has spinal meningitis. If they don't find it in the early stages, there is no hope."

But God!

I asked numerous times if I could go home, but the doctor met my requests with resistance. Dr. Susan would not discharge me until she knew what was wrong with me. The hospital stay affected my mind (what little I have) so much that I thought the pastor's son and the Braswell boys were putting poison in my food.

Finally, the day before my birthday, they let me go home after spending three weeks in the hospital. God was, and is, my only answer. I still think of it every time I get a slight headache.

Some of the Nelms family were there every day. Hazel stayed every night and almost every day. I appreciate all everyone did.

But God brought me out of it.

# Another Tornado

A tornado came through the Valdosta area sometime in the afternoon. I sat at my den window and watched it lay a large pine tree on neighbor Bobby Johnson's house next door. They weren't home.

A large dead pine tree between our house and his was left standing straight and tall. The storm lifted over our house and set down again in the garden, laying corn in every direction.

"I believe God likes you," someone said.

I know He does. I love Him so much.

I'm looking forward to being part of His bride when He comes to take us home.

# The Quilt

In my younger adult life, I took painting lessons. I loved to paint birds and scenery. I painted birds on the top cabinet doors in my travel trailer kitchen in 1978.

Many years later, I made quilts to give away as gifts, but I kept the prettiest one I ever made. It was white, pink, and green. The first top block said "Jesus" in pink paint. There were 31 more hand-painted blocks with words that described Jesus, including "Comforter," "Healer," "Light," and more. I also painted birds on it.

After I told the people at the funeral home about it, they wanted to buy it for a drawing. I initially refused, but they kept on until I let them have it for $200. At that time, we were trying hard to pay off the church mortgage. I put the money on the church.

An older couple in assisted living won the quilt in the funeral home's drawing. They loved it. When they went to bed at night, the quilt covered them. People thought the couple loved the painted birds. I believe they wanted the painted words covering them.

I thought I could make another quilt just like it. I got the blocks cut for the wording and the words written on and painted. When I started to do the birds, all the pictures of birds I had saved for years were missing. I had cleaned the house and burned a lot of trash and things we thought we'd never need again. I must have burned them by mistake.

After 20 years, I still have 32 painted blocks in a Ziplock bag. I have forgotten how the quilt was set together. I don't have the quilt from which I copied it and we have lost the picture book of quilts.

The quilt the old couple loved so much was put on top of one of their caskets and then put inside and buried with it.

Because they loved it so.

# Jocelynn's Mystery

David Stone took his children down the creek in a canoe about a mile from his house. It was a beautiful day, and all were happy. Suddenly, they hit a rock and the canoe flipped. His little girl, Jocelynn, was pinned under it. David tried but couldn't lift the canoe. He saw a foot and dragged her out. Apparently too late. He turned her on her face and tried to pump the water out.

A nurse who David didn't know was floating down in another canoe. She rushed to help. Someone called 911. After about 20 minutes, Jocelynn took a breath. And then another. She woke up in the hospital with her Aunt Meme sitting beside her.

"Meme, I saw Daddy's mama," Jocelynn said.

No one had ever talked to her about Wanda, her daddy's mother who died when David was six months old. How did she know at six years old that David ever had a mother? There were no pictures. David's stepmother destroyed all of them. No one talked of Wanda to the seven children she left. It was too painful.

Yet, Wanda's granddaughter knew her at six years old when she was in a coma.

Only a mystery and a miracle of God

# Linda

Hazel broke her hip and we learned during her stay in the hospital that she had colon cancer. She lived just 15 months after that.

Linda and Rita Kay came for the funeral, which was held on a Friday, one day before a tornado hit the area and caused destruction. The mess forced church to be canceled, so I asked Pastor Nelms to come to our house for service.

Linda, my oldest daughter, was backslidden for 45 years. and was already trying to make her way back home before our house service. But she stayed.

Pastor Nelms preached. Linda went for it all the way with all her heart. It's been more than four years and she is still going forward.

Never give up on anyone. It seemed like all hope for Linda was gone.

But if there is life, there is hope.

# I'm Here for a Purpose

After Jesus saved my life from the stove incident, we started attending church in Valdosta. We lived 40 miles away in Lee, Florida.

Many changes have come in the past 30 years. There have been 24 family deaths and many friends have passed away. I was older than all of them but one.

God has brought me back to Valdosta Church for a purpose. I am 92. I can't hear good, unless God speaks. I certainly want to hear Him. My smelling is gone. My seeing is dim. I've told on myself so much for the crazy things I do such as falling after jumping on a board with both feet to break it.

Now, the pastor won't allow me on a step ladder. That takes all the fun out of life. I can't feed the birds. I can't wash my windows. I can't hang my pictures, turn on the ceiling fans, fix my curtain rods, or paint the kitchen. Next, I won't be allowed to lie on the bed or couch because I might fall off. They tell me to sit down and look pretty. I can't do that because I looked in the mirror. I don't know what it is, but God has a purpose.

Help me Jesus to fulfill that purpose quickly so I don't have to sit and feel sorry for myself. It is much easier mentally to work than to sit and wish I could.

Maybe if the pastor and others would turn me loose and let me try, I would soon learn I can't do it anymore anyway.

# Three Hours, Not One

Will you pray one hour? I heard pastor say.
But I haven't the time. I can't do it today.
My day is so full, 'til the time is all gone.
With work of this world, I keep on the run.

Maybe just a half hour? Can you give that for prayer?
Give heart, soul and being, for my Jesus does care.
Oh! I keep Him in my mind as I go on my way.
He understands I just can't do it today.

Tomorrow, I'll try to take time for prayer.
For I know if I follow, He'll always be there.
Tomorrow may not come. Won't you come to Him now?
He'll meet you today if you'll only bow.

Jesus went to the garden in Matthew we see.
Not just one hour, but Jesus had three.
Tarry here and watch while I go and pray.
But they all fell asleep. They'd had a hard day.

Can't you just watch one hour, Jesus said on return.
His heart was so heavy. They had so much to learn.
Come let us be going He told them that day.
He gave will to the spirit as they led Him away.

The pastor is not asking too much.

# My Friend

Sometimes it's easy for people I know
To meet new friends everywhere that they go.
They laugh and they chatter, and talk on and on,
Just like they were old friends who had never been gone.

They don't meet a stranger.
Just new friends they say.
Friend from all over
When they've just met today.

But I've had a problem all my life through.
I don't like to meet people; the old ones will do.
I'd get me a friend, and for dear life I'd hang on
'Cause a friend I'd not have if this friend were gone.

I'd try to be with them everywhere they would go,
Because that's my friend and I care for them so.
I'd try to give all down to my last dime,
If only they'd let me be there all the time

Nothing else mattered but pleasing my friend.
Then I'd end up heartbroken and alone in the end.
I'd say, now I've learned my lesson for sure.
Then someone else comes along and I just ask for more.

But one thing I've learned, there is one true Friend.
And that friend is Jesus. He'll stay to the end.
I can give Him my all, down to my last dime.
If I give Him my heart, He'll be there all the time.

# COVID-19

Everyone told me to wear a mask when COVID-19 hit. But I couldn't. My breathing is bad from working on the chicken farms for too many years. I can't get enough oxygen through a mask.

Stay home?

Not from church. I'd trust God instead.

My best earthly friends live in Fitzgerald. After staying home for months, we decided to go visit them in their home. We started the 80-mile trip. It started sprinkling. The farther we went, the harder it rained. We turned around and started home. The rain quit. If we had continued, we would have met with COVID-19 head on.

We went to a funeral in Fitzgerald with our pastor's family. We had a gift for my best friend's soon-to-be granddaughter. My friend texted me and said she was feeling poorly. We didn't take the gift. It turns out, she had COVID-19. Their whole church had it. Thank you, Jesus, we escaped again.

My family next door got COVID-19. I asked them not to come over until it died down a bit. I didn't want it. The father worked on a public job. I knew he could carry it home and he did. Brenda was home because of other ailments. She got covid and died with it. I never even got to see her, except by FaceTime. I escaped again.

I planned a trip to Arkansas to celebrate birthdays for me and my great-great granddaughter. We share a birthday and have never been together on it. Just before time to go, they had another round of Covid-19. They got it again. We stayed home.

"I believe God loves you," people would say to me.

I know He does, and I love Him.

It's been two years since I started running from COVID-19. Thank you, Jesus. I'll keep running with You holding my hand.

# Tomorrow About this Time

I usually go to church to pray early every morning except on Sundays when we all go together at 10. Barbara goes with me. I felt God wanted me to do that.

I didn't have gas money one week.

"Jesus, help me." I said.

Ordinarily, I keep the tank at least half full. I went to pray every morning and the hand in my gas gauge never dropped. It went down a little when I made a trip to town. It dropped a little as usual when we went to church. I had money coming in the first of the month. The gas hand never got below half. That's my God!

One morning, I walked around the church praying and asking God to save my son Charles. He is my only birth child. He needed baptism in Jesus' name, and he needs the Holy Ghost. He needed healing for his sick body. He needed to get rid of his hate for his daddy who left him at five months.

He was baptized at 10 years old to please his grandmother. He loved her very much and thought that would make her happy. I was praying so hard for him that morning. Oh, Jesus, save him.

As I passed the window on the right side of the church, God spoke. I just know He did.

"Tomorrow about this time," He said.

Oh, how I prayed. The next morning while walking in about the same spot, the phone rang. I remembered "Tomorrow about this time." It was Charles. He was crying, lonely, sick, and wanted his mama. He was sorry for the life he had lived. He kept calling me "Mama."

He hadn't called me Mama since he was a very small child. After he was grown, it was "Mother." I talked to him. I prayed with him. I went to see him and spent one night. He confessed a lot of wrongs and said he wanted to do right.

I don't believe that God spoke for just that one phone call. There must be more I can do. I didn't bring one child into this world to be lost in a burning hell.

I know God was in it.

God help us.

# Restrictions

I love my Jesus with all my heart.
It's been that way right from the start.
When I heard of my Maker, and His love divine,
I wanted to serve Him with joy. He is mine.

I loved to travel. No place was too far.
If I had money for gas, I ran my own car.
But my body says no. You can't make it that way.
Just forget it, stay home, and be happy today.

I'll just do some sewing. I have plenty to do.
Make a dress, or a quilt before I get through.
But my back is soon tired. I can't sit very long.
So back to the recliner is where I belong.

I really would like to fix up the house,
Put on some sheet rock to shut out that mouse.
But that's takes a ladder, which makes me to cry.
My pastor won't let me. I can't understand why.

I can get on a stepstool, paint can or chair.
With nothing to hold to, I stand in midair.
When I have a good ladder and I hang on tight
But he shakes his head and says that's not right.

To take my ladder, and keep it from me
Is like taking a monkey away from a tree.
The squirrels that jump from tree to tree
They all seem so happy with no care, they're free.

**The church where it all began for me. God has been so good to me. It's a great life living for the Lord. Thank you, Jesus!**

www.ingramcontent.com/pod-product-compliance
Lightning Source LLC
LaVergne TN
LVHW050628100826
845148LV00011B/1781